Fiery Learning from the Pastoral Front Line

Darline Joseph Marianathan

ISBN 978-1-78222-953-7

Book design, layout and production management by Into Print
www.intoprint.net
+44 (0)1604 832140

A note from Archbishop Mark O'Toole

I commend this book of Reflections by Fr Darline. Most of them first appeared in public print in the Parish or the local newspaper. They indicate Fr Darline's capacity to reach out to his parishioners and indeed more widely to all the local community. They speak of faith and the important things in life.

What is especially precious is Fr Darline's love of the Lord and his love of God's holy people. Both of these are well testified in these reflections. These past two years we have all been living within the limits of COVID and the reflections captured here reflect this reality, too. But they do so with a sense of hope and the power of the human spirit, of the importance of community, and the fidelity of God to those who seek His face. Also, particularly original and creative is Fr Darline's background in psychology. He wears his expertise lightly, introducing it in order to give a fresh insight into a particular issue.

I am sure that you will enjoy reading Fr Darline's reflections. I congratulate him on this achievement in the midst of a busy pastoral and academic life. May what he has written bring each of us closer to the Lord who is so good to us.

With my kindest wishes

+Mark O'Toole

Archbishop of Cardiff

Bishop of Menevia

Message from Canon Paul Cummins

As a fellow priest in the pastoral front line of the Diocese of Plymouth, I recognise much of what Fr Darline writes in these reflections. We have come through a time of intense change on so many levels, and these reflections illustrate how Father Darline and the people of Okehampton & Chagford have responded in so many creative ways. When I first met Fr Darline many years ago in Exeter, I saw in him an enthusiasm for pastoral ministry in the Church, and a deep desire to reach out to any who are in need of healing. His study of psychology has helped develop his many pastoral gifts, and his integrative approach to health and wellbeing has further enhanced his pastoral ministry. Father Darline has always been very keen on the use of technology to reach out to both parishioners and the wider world. In doing so he gives a great example of how we can all use our talents in furthering the mission of the Church to proclaim the healing love of God.

Canon Paul Cummins
Diocesan Administrator
Diocese of Plymouth

Foreword

I'm not sure anyone in this diocese needs me to tell them what a gift they have in Darline Marianathan.

I have worked with Darline for several years now, sadly all of it online, though I hope that will change. In reading his stories of life in the parish both before, during and after the height of the pandemic, I can feel his respect for his parishioners and his love for the job and the people he serves.

I am not a resident of the parish and I know him in a different capacity: as a psychotherapist and supervisor, overseeing his clinical work as he strives to complete his Doctoral studies. I'm not quite sure how he does it, how he does his job as a pastor so well and yet completes his assignments, while also working as a clinician for several hours each week beyond his parish.

He has written about his difficulty finding a placement, that there is a resistance to his being a Catholic priest. I believe these organisations are doing themselves a disservice. As you are aware, your parish priest is compassionate and non-judgemental, clear in his own mind on questions of morality and virtue, but also willing to accept the frailty in others. He is kind. I also witnessed his unstinting willingness during the pandemic to visit parishioners who were gravely ill. He did this despite his own anxieties concerning covid, his fear of coming down with the virus himself, which he did on several occasions.

St Boniface is a parish which, by all accounts, has thrived under Darline's stewardship. During the recent lockdowns he continued to say mass, to provide counsel and encouragement, and to tend to his flock despite the obstacles and the enforcement of personal distance. He also worked as a psychotherapist, none of his clients were aware that he was also a priest. Some of you may not have known that he is also a psychotherapist?

Darline came to you when he was young – only 31 years of age. He has grown up with you and, as he looks after his parishioners, I know that you will also look after him. Take a leaf out of my book and yell at him whenever you think he is not looking after himself to the extent that he needs to do to look after you. Good food and love, and lots of sleep. Oh, and let's not forget a sense of humour, an attribute your pastor has in abundance. Dedication, courage, intelligence, and good humour. They don't come better than that.

Dr Marie Adams
Psychotherapy/Training/Supervision

Senior Lecturer
Metanoia Institute
London

Introduction

It is both a pleasure and a privilege to write an introduction for Darline Joseph Marianathan's latest literary work. He is truly a Renaissance figure, well versed in the humanities and scientific outlook as is witnessed by his many degrees in science and psychology.

I have had the pleasure of knowing him for several years now and I continue to be amazed at his ability to write with so much insight and compassion of the human condition, and his success as a much-loved parish priest. Pre-Covid, the parish was a star of the Plymouth diocese with its many activities, all to encourage us to see ourselves as a community, a family of God. As we emerge from the pandemic, he is again encouraging activities such as a parish lunch and also plans to mark the centenary of Saint Boniface church Okehampton.

His knowledge of IT has also produced a diocesan much envied webpage and, as the following case studies show, his devotion to the priesthood and his parishioners take first place for him.

I hope you will enjoy reading his case studies and that they will enlighten your mind and spiritual self.

Dr Marie A Mills *C.Pschol., AFBPsS., Csci.,MBACP (senior status),*
UKRC, BPS Registered Psychologist Specialising in Psychotherapy Senior
status (ROPSIP)

Acknowledgements

I am extremely grateful to Archbishop Mark O' Toole for his introductory note with its encouragement and support. With his support and help I have been able to continue both my ministry and study satisfactorily.

Canon Paul Cummins was the first person I met 13 years ago at Exeter University, even before I met with Bishop Christopher Budd when I was exploring the possibility of my ministry in the Diocese. Since then, he has been a huge support and help to me both pastorally and academically. My thanks to him for his words of appreciation and for his encouragement with this book.

The foreword from Dr Marie Adams summarises not only the contents of the book but also brings out what a wonderful humanity she has in herself. She carries over two decades of work experience with the BBC and several years of psychotherapy teaching and practise. I have been so fortunate to learn from her wealth of knowledge and experience and I am so grateful for this.

Dr Marie Mills and I have spoken about the undisputable fact that it was God's plan that we meet each other. She is not only a successful academic with several publications to her name, but also a fantastic therapist. I am lucky to have known her for over a decade and really blessed to have worked very closely with her for the past five years. Marie has a powerful presence, with grace and guidance. It is mainly with her help and input that I was able to find my 'true self' and grow 'whole, grounded and steady'. Thanks to Marie for the fantastic introduction.

The people of Okehampton and Chagford, both Catholics and non-Catholics, have been a huge source of inspiration for this book. Many thanks to you all.

Special thanks to Dr Justine Frain, Nicola Whitehead and Monica Soby who have edited and corrected the text. Thanks to Mr Guru and Remo Reegan for the fantastic art works.

Thanks also to Mark Webb from Paragon Publishers for his patience and professionalism in bringing this book to fruition on time.

Darline Joseph Marianathan

Dedication

To the people of Okehampton & Chagford

Contents

---

1   All the names in this chapter are anonymised at the request of the family
members.

1. My Ministry during COVID 19

The whole world was beginning to feel the weight of the Pandemic and a number of stringent measures had been announced, including a travel ban. I had travelled to India on 2 March 2020 to attend my father's funeral since he died on 1 March. After a week in India I booked for 18th March to return to Britain but British Airways cancelled my ticket due to the increasing concern about COVID in England. I wrote to Bishop Mark about my difficulties and, as usual, he was kind and supportive in reply. Most of the countries throughout the world were closing air travel and many, including India, were announcing repatriation schemes to enable their own citizens working and living overseas to get back. It seemed people were rushing in all directions. While many Indians from overseas were trying to come back, I was trying to get out of India to come to Britain. I re-booked my ticket for 20th March, and this was also cancelled, but I managed to get a flight on 22nd March and landed at last at Heathrow Terminal 5, which looked unusually empty with only a few travellers moving around.

My mother and the rest of my family were not very pleased with my decision to fly back to Britain and the Indian media wasn't paying as much attention to the virus as the British media. I had left my iPad with my nieces and nephews so they could watch a couple of BBC documentaries and they saw the BBC News about the pandemic as it was breaking from the UK. My mother, influenced by my nieces and nephews, did not approve my travel adventure, but I managed to convince her with the hope of my plans to return within the next six months. However, with the prolonged pandemic this wouldn't happen for well over a year.

I was getting some sense of the seriousness of the virus from the BBC News although not fully. I remember reading the news from India on 20th March 2020 when Prime Minister Boris Johnson announced the need to shut down all cafes, pubs, restaurants, nightclubs, theatres, cinemas, gyms and leisure centres. The following day there was another news item about shoppers who were panic buying and, as a result, supermarkets around the UK were struggling to keep up with demand. This didn't deter my plan to travel to Britain, although I also knew I was still grieving for my beloved father and was feeling sorry for my loving mother. I had, nevertheless, a compelling feeling of the need to be present for the needs of my parishioners in Okehampton and Chagford.

I was fortunate to have studied at St. Peter's Pontifical seminary where there were veteran priests like Father Lucian Legrand, a French missionary, who had learned Tamil and lived the life of the ordinary people there. He was an intelligent scripture scholar and at the same time, a simple person who taught us about how a priest needs to be. Ever since my time at this seminary, I've had a strong feeling in me of being called to be a *martyr* and a *saviour*. This conviction was strengthened after my university studies in Britain where I was fortunate to graduate from Exeter and Bristol universities with MSc and MEd (BPS) Psychology Degrees respectively. All these studies and the 15 years of pastoral ministry in the parishes, particularly the last 10 years in Okehampton and Chagford, have strengthened my resolve to be a priest for the people and the place. I think this conviction was behind my decision to come back from India to Britain at the start of the pandemic.

Everything, including the churches, seemed to be closing down in Britain. We swiftly decided to move all our services online, one of the first Parishes in the area to do so. It was relatively easy for us since we had been live-streaming services since 2011 for our housebound parishioners. With the help of some of our "IT-savvy" parishioners we were able to ensure that almost the entire Catholic community of Okehampton and Chagford was online – just 18 parishioners were not. We used Skype, Facetime and Zoom in the beginning, which was great when everything went well, but it was a difficult challenge whenever there was a problem with one of the apps or devices. With the help of remote hosts, I managed to hold the services by myself, while handling three devices (laptop, iPad and a mobile phone) on the altar. At one point there were 179 devices connected to our apps. I must confess the quality of the service was not as good as it would be under normal circumstances, but we survived. There was not a single instance when we had to cancel the service. Even when there was a network problem, a couple of non-Catholics at Okehampton generously gave me their mobile phones to be used for hotspot wifi sharing.

The Caritas from the Catholic Diocese of Plymouth used our Parish for a case study in their magazine published in October 2020 (6th edition). Most of our meetings moved to online platforms, which put more pressure on me personally. At the start of the Pandemic, there were numerous calls from people around the country, plus four requests from USA and Australia, to do online prayers for the sick. These were people who had visited our Parish in the past and had been following our swift shift to online services via our website. I was busier than ever - visiting the sick in hospitals and care homes, wearing full PPE (Personal Protective Equipment), getting ready for complete lockdown, doing services with restricted numbers when the lockdowns ended and trying to convince people to volunteer to be stewards. At times it all seemed too much. I was ringing around to check if house-bound Parishioners who are not online were alright and I think I picked up their anxiety. I had to self-isolate five times and eventually caught the virus myself during which I experienced the kindness and the generosity of our Parishioners. There were times when I felt depressed and was scared of being killed by the virus. However, I managed to survive. Personal prayer and personal psychological therapy (a million thanks to Dr. Marie Mills) were key to my continued existence during the pandemic.

Father Darline at St. Boniface Okehampton on Sunday 23rd May 2021

There were calls from every direction for the help of my pastoral skills and psychological knowledge. Although we are a small parish, we had lots of social activities involving every age group prior to COVID 19 which had all had to stop. This was having a huge impact on the mental health of our Parishioners so I decided to keep the technical devices and the connecting apps going so that people could interact with each other for about 20 minutes before and after the services. This helped people to speak to one another and catch up on things. I started to give talks online on mental health. The Zoom masses every weekend had some notable scenes as backdrop, including St. Peter's Square, the Holy Land, Niagara Falls and the seven wonders of the world, including the Taj Mahal, which cheered our parishioners.

In addition, there were requests from the town to write into the local newspapers about how we can maintain our mental wellbeing during the pandemic. I have been writing in the local newspapers now for the last 10 years but trying to write during COVID 19 was a huge challenge. Of the 18 newspaper articles I wrote during the pandemic, 12 of them were about how to keep ourselves mentally healthy. The first article I wrote during COVID 19 was inspired by Pope Francis' idea of the 'creativity of love' which appeared on 9th April 2020 (see below).

Surviving COVID-19 through Holy Week and Easter

Our Churches, both St. Boniface at Okehampton and the Holy Family at Chagford, are usually packed with people during Holy Week and Easter. The richness of piety during Holy Week and the joy of celebration at Easter are profound for all those who usually come to the services. Certainly, this year it was very different, and yet the usual message of hope and the need for calm in the midst of panic and despair remained of paramount importance.

The outbreak of this COVID-19 pandemic has brought the world to a standstill. The day-by-day and ever-increasing numbers of global infection and death are alarming. Medical and health experts are in utter dismay and disbelief at the jet speed spread of this virus. They openly acknowledge their struggles at the herculean task of finding a potential cure and effective vaccination for this invisible killer in the near future. The sheer force of collateral damage to human lives and the global economy puts the public in panic mode. People are frightened and confused.

All countries in the world are trying to fight this pandemic through all possible means. So far the most common method of response for most countries, including ours, seems to be lockdown. It is neither a permanent solution nor a cure, but the only available choice at the moment to buy time until more robust alternative approaches to save lives are identified. Under the present climate no one is certain how long this lockdown will continue. It is no fun to be prisoners in our own houses for weeks on end, especially when the weather is becoming warmer, something we have been desperately awaiting all these months. Staying indoors for long periods, without the usual access to people and places we love most, is frustrating and upsetting. Such a scenario is usually a strong contributor to our mental and physical ill health. On top of that, the increased airtime the media has these days for COVID-19, with graphic demonstrations of mounting infection and death statistics, adds to the stress, anxiety and panic that we find difficult to manage presently.

Certainly, the public needs to be informed and concerned about the seriousness of the situation, so that necessary precautions are in place to stop the spread of this contagion. However, airing unhelpful information should be avoided to aid our survival in isolation and stop setting viewers in perpetual panic mode. To enhance our life of 'social distancing' and 'isolation' during Holy Week, Pope Francis's message recommends engaging in 'creativity of love' that can increase our hope and keep us healthy and calm as individuals and families. In these uncertain times while our politicians, police, researchers, medical professionals and volunteers are doing their best to get us out of this peril, let us continue to pray like the Psalmist: "Yes, my soul, find rest in God; my hope comes from him. Truly, he is my rock and my salvation. He is my fortress; I will not be shaken" (Ps 62: 5-6).

The above write up was much appreciated by many. Some wrote to me expressing gratitude and appreciation but wondering about my struggles in coping with the virus. Many of my parishioners and some of those in the area who know me, are aware I am an outdoor person and they all wondered if I was alright, given the self-isolation I had to undergo after returning from India. Therefore, I decided to go public with my style of coping, which I thought might help some readers. I wrote the following piece which was published on 7th May 2020.

Staying healthy and happy during the COVID-19 outbreak

My thoughts and prayers go out to those who have died of the virus, but I am equally concerned about those who, like me, are struggling to cope with this precarious situation.

We are so lucky to have well organised voluntary groups in this part of the country, caring neighbours and fantastic friends who go out of their way to help those of us in need. In this article, I want to share my own experience of coping at this challenging time, which some readers might find helpful.

I rushed back from India after the loss of my own father earlier in March, while still in mourning for him and I had to put myself in self-isolation. For someone with a personality like mine, who is also an outdoors person, it was pretty unbearable at the beginning; the internet went down, the phone line collapsed, and the heating would go off every half hour. After a couple of days when the phone and the internet were reinstated, I was flooded with a tsunami of sadness and grief from the isolation. There were over 40 requests from people of our Parish and visitors for prayers for those who had died or were suffering seriously with COVID-19 or other illness. In addition, the demands of isolation meant there were no visits to parishioners, even for emergencies. Sadly, during this time two of our devout parishioners passed away. One of the riches of my Pastoral ministry, which I will always cherish, is to have accompanied dying parishioners in the last minutes of their earthly life, but at this time I was forbidden from that noble ministry. Although I moved on to doing services online, it is still very difficult to manage the lack of emotional connections with the physical presence of people and places.

I have become aware of the need for inner strength to survive this situation. Certainly the 10 tips from the NHS can help us survive

COVID-19 but beyond these it is my faith that kept, and still keeps, sustaining me. I remember that someone once said to me "Faith is like wifi. It is invisible but it has the power to connect you." Interestingly these days it is wifi that is connecting our faith.

I personally believe we all need faith at the moment... Faith in our system, medical professionals, police, politicians and ultimately in God to keep us all safe and healthy at this time of challenge and difficulty. "Faith is the assurance of things hoped for, the conviction of things not seen" (Hebrews 11:1).

The above article was as well received as the previous one. I was pleased to know that some found my article empowering since I had been open about my vulnerability and how I managed to cope with the uncertainty of the time. As we were emerging out of the first lockdown there were concerns about the new normal and so I wrote the following piece published on 4ᵗʰ June 2020.

Our new normal greeting might well be the Tamil way

Significant information is emerging almost every day from the medical and scientific community about the killer virus COVID-19, though a cure and a vaccine seem to be far off. Countries are copying coping and have their own containment strategies. Contact tracing is the latest approach that we in the UK have learned from countries such as Singapore, Hong Kong and Germany, who have been successfully using this for a while.

It is a relief to notice the relatively slow and the non-linear progression of the infection and death toll of the virus within our region, compared with other areas in the UK. Long-term lockdown is predicted to have a devastating impact on our economy and our wellbeing. Therefore, there is a pressing need to ease the lockdown, even if not fully, then at least in stages, depending upon the spread of the virus. However, there is a strong medical prediction that for some time we may not be able to greet our family, friends and acquaintances in the usual way with handshakes, hugs and kisses. COVID-19 is understood to be a social virus and as likely to spread by touch as by coughing or sneezing. We however, are used to expressing care, warmth and interest in each other through touch.

The feeling of warm touch increases the level of oxytocin in the brain; this is involved in strengthening social bonds and trust in relationships. At the face of this precarious contagion, we are left with no choice other than to invent or copy a new way to meet and greet people. As all our Church services are now online with Zoom, FaceTime and Skype, I seem to have adopted a Tamil way of greeting people with Vanakam (Hello in Tamil); this is similar to Namaste in Hindi. For those who are interested, Tamil is a classical language and has a very ancient and independent tradition, with a considerable body of ancient literature. The most revered ancient text (from 300 BCE) is Tirukkural, which has been translated into at least 42 world languages, with about 57 different renderings in the English language alone. Leo Tolstoy held it in high esteem for its universality and secular nature.

A Tamil's way of greeting is usually done by uttering the word Vanakam while holding both hands with palms and fingers gently pushed against each other. 'Vana' means 'vanangu' (worship) and 'ak' represents the Tamil alphabet '∴' meaning human eyes along with the third eye- God. When spoken Vanakam with the hand posture as mentioned above, it is believed that the person is greeted as a sign of respect for being the person he/she is, as well as an acknowledgement of God's presence within that person. In many ways it is a spiritual greeting not confined to any religion.

In the upcoming new normal scenario, we may not be able to shake hands, hug or kiss each other for a while, but we certainly can greet each other with Vanakam both on- and offline. This word may not have the power to increase the level of oxytocin but will certainly boost the other happy neurotransmitters - dopamine, serotonin, and endorphins. Vanakam to you all.

The above article also received the same level of attention as the others I had written. In the midst of the pandemic, there was a big issue with the use of the algorithm in GCSE and A-Level assessments and children of some of the people I know have been affected by this. Although the whole issue came to an amicable end, I decided to write about it with the intention of highlighting the need to hold algorithm in a more sensible way in the future than the way it is used presently. This was published on 27th August 2020.

The power of humans and the algorithm

There has been so much noise in recent days about the Ofqual exam results algorithm. Public outcry, debate and student protest have now ensured the sensible use of teachers' assessments for GCSE and A-level results. I felt so relieved when the government and Ofqual at last relented to public pleas, unlike our Indian government, which is using a similar approach to bring in a new nationwide educational system known as the New Education Policy (NEP).

One of the mistakes spotted in the algorithm's calculations was associated with users' lack of understanding of mathematics during the data input.

As a student of advanced statistics, I used to scratch my head sometimes, especially when the output was totally rubbish and incompatible with the input data. Anyone who has worked with computers knows the expression "rubbish in, rubbish out", and this will reflect how the algorithm operated. Common sense and conscious reflective thinking - two distinct characteristics of humans - are incompatible with an algorithm. This is the major difference between humans and algorithms.

Algorithms are mechanical and incredibly useful. They are involved in almost everything we use today including our computers, digital apps, GPS mapping and artificial intelligence. However, for best results there is a need for an efficient and capable human being to direct its operation. Humans are not free from errors, bias, and prejudice, but unlike algorithms civilised humans are more likely to employ a sense of competence, justice and sympathy on conscientious grounds. That is the reason that teachers' assessment is welcome news at this challenging time.

It is not about whether the algorithm or human ability is best. It is about how well we bring these two together for the good of all, not just a select few.

"You shall do no injustice in court. You shall not be partial to the poor or defer to the great, but in righteousness shall you judge your neighbour" (Leviticus 19:15).

Following the above article, there was a compelling need to reflect why staying at home was becoming too difficult. The public was asked to stay at home with an extended lockdown in order to keep the rise of infection rate low. It was personally difficult for me too to accept the extended lockdown but there was no other option than to stick to the rule. The following write up published on 21st January 2021 was an invitation to the public to understand why we all find it hard now to stay at home.

Why staying at home is hard?

Both national and local police keep reminding people to stay at home to help minimise the infection rate and deaths from this pandemic. More than 30,000 fines have been handed out for COVID-19 breaches so far. I hear many people express how hard it is to stay at home for so long. Despite being a practicing psychologist, at times I find that my own level of motivation to stay at home is shaky. I am an outdoor person and I was getting tired of this 'stay at home' advice, aware too of the physical and psychological damage of enforced isolation. On the other hand, I know that there is no other way to stop the exponentially swelling infection rate. One of the ways I managed to soothe these feelings was to deepen my understanding of why staying at home is becoming harder.

"Home is the starting place of love, hope and dreams".

"Home is where love resides, memories are created, friends always belong, and laughter never ends."

There are thousands of such quotes about the indispensable part that homes play in our life.

We have evolved around the social and cultural practice of staying in one place most of the time, leaving home for work during the day and coming back home at night. This practice has undergone a huge change in recent years. We move around a lot more. We like to move house, change cars, jobs and sometimes relationships. The desire for 'forward' change seems to be the mantra for happy living. This present pandemic has imposed a 'backward' change on us, pushing us to go back to our old ways, with far more restrictions. This almost sounds as if we are being imprisoned in our own houses. This is hard, but there does not appear to be a better way than this if we want to keep ourselves and others safe and escape this invisible killer. "Do not let your hearts be troubled. You believe in God; believe also in me" (John 14:1).

I received a few letters commenting on the above write up. One letter said, "I bet it will not be too long before you write about the need to get out of the house." That reader was correct. Although the infection rate was not slowing down as expected, the death rate was declining. However, I noticed I had a lot of anxiety within me, as did many of the parishioners and people in the area, in spite of having had two vaccinations. Therefore, I wrote the following reflection that was published on 15th July 2021.

Think Positive

While we are still in the midst of the COVID 19 pandemic, the word 'positive' sounds rather scary and negative. I have felt lots of positive energy myself as I noticed the colours and enthusiasm at the Devon County Show and the England team's most enthralling victories at the Euro 2020 football matches over the last few weeks.

The prolonged suffocation caused by the threat of exposure to COVID-19 infection, and associated fear of death, certainly hurts our economy, but also damages our entire psyche. I have heard and seen the harm caused by this repeated and unprecedented exposure in my roles as shepherd of our parishioners and as a psychologist.

It is important to follow all the safety instructions in order to keep both ourselves and others free of COVID-19 but the prolonged nature of anxious thoughts about catching the virus and dying of it is more dangerous than the actual virus. Many of us seem to suffer from a fear of catching the virus, and I must confess I used to be one of them.

One of the ways I rebuilt my resilience towards this challenging situation was to bring in positive thoughts that are realistic. I used to say to myself that, as I have had two jabs, wear masks and gloves in other peoples' presence and maintain social distancing, I shouldn't be too concerned about catching the virus. Even if I were to catch the virus, I feel confident I can fight it off. More importantly, I made it a point to listen to the news about COVID-19 just once a day and focus on news happening in and around the town, the country and the world for the rest of the time.

I have heard from many people who feel better by adopting this way of functioning. People who believe in God and prayer also feel even better as they go about their lives with less anxiety and more energy. "Rejoice in hope, be patient in tribulation, be constant in prayer" Romans 12: 12.

The above reflections are a few examples of how I managed to cope as well as help others to survive the challenges of the COVID 19 pandemic.

2. My ongoing journey

When I first arrived at St. Boniface, Okehampton on Thursday 3rd November 2011, I said that Bishop Christopher Budd had saved my vocation. My life before then was a time of discernment about whether to continue to be a priest or not, but the welcome by the people of Okehampton and Chagford was so warm and good that the decision to continue my life as a priest got strengthened.

However, I could sense an anxious feeling in the air for some parishioners, and I felt the same within myself. This was understandable as I was the first non-European priest in the 100-year history of the Parish. I very soon began to feel at ease however, with huge support from the then Dean Canon John Deeny and Canon Paul Cummins, the Episcopal Vicar for clergy and Mgr. Harry Doyle, the Diocesan Finance department manager. Developing relationships with other local clergy in the area wasn't difficult either, although it took some effort to start with.

I was lucky in many ways since Canon Peter Morgan had laid a good foundation at all levels in the Parish. People had been informed of my arrival, so there was no huge surprise. The sacramental and the catechetical parts of the Parish were well organised, and this enabled me to get straight on with my ministry. I was happy to continue with things as they were, and I thought the priority was to get to know the parishioners and people around me. This was a little difficult to start with, given the cultural differences, but it wasn't an onerous task since as a missionary priest I was mentally prepared to love the people and place wherever I was sent. The seeds of faith had been sown early in my mind, firstly by my parents and then by the good nuns and priests of India. In India we have a long history of European missionaries bringing faith to ordinary people like me. Along with faith, these missionaries democratised education, healthcare and livelihoods, which would never have been possible for the majority of Indians like me.

Catholic faith influenced lots of Indians to challenge the oppressive social structures. One such was Periyar E.V. Ramasamy (1879 – 1973). He was a Tamil Indian social activist who championed rationalism, self-respect and women's rights, and in 1947 begged the British not to abandon Indians to perpetual slavery through Independence. He pleaded: "Please continue to rule us, even if you have to do so from Britain, rather than abandoning us into the hands of the higher castes from whom freedom is impossible". He said this because of the inhuman ideology in a higher caste Indian religions that justified treating the lower castes as untouchables. This was the reason for his public repudiation of North Indian gods. He was aware of the detriments of colonisation, but compared to what he saw and experienced, he preferred colonial rule to the unfair treatment of the dehumanising caste system. Colonisation and Christianity brought Indian women freedom from sati, eradicated female infanticide, encouraged widow remarriage, promoted health care and democratised education for all castes, which had previously been reserved for the higher castes only.

Without the impact of the Catholic faith as introduced by the European missionaries, India would have been 100 years behind where it is today. The missionaries I feel most deeply connected to are the Italian-born Jesuit priest, Joseph Beschi (1680- 1742), the Irish born Congregational missionary Robert Caldwell (1814-1891) and the Canadian Lutheran missionary G U Pope (1820-1908) whose father was from Padstow, Cornwall. These people went to my homeland Tamilnadu for missionary service. They started to learn Tamil for their missionary work but ended up exploring and sharing the rich treasures of the Tamil language and its classically opulent literature with the world. Their discoveries, research and contributions have been acknowledged by UNESCO and the Indian Government.

Before coming to Britain, I had done my homework and was pleasantly surprised to know how, as in India, this entire nation was shaped by Catholic faith. The significant role played by the Catholic clergy in this country is known through the historical connections between Roman Britain and the Catholic Christendom dating back to the 1st century. There are historical records that reveal how at the start of the 6th century Augustine of Canterbury, sent by Pope Gregory, played a huge role in establishing monasteries and providing education to the monks and the local residents. This continued throughout Anglo-Saxon and Norman conquests during which monasteries and convents became a vital part of the society, pioneering education, healthcare and lodging for the general public. Popes Gregory IX, Nicholas IV and John XXII offered universities like Oxford and Cambridge legal protection and status to compete with other medieval universities in Europe. This paved the way for Archbishop Walter de Merton to establish Merton College at Oxford, which still holds a strong reputation for academic excellence. Many Catholic clergy took residence in both universities and maintained a high level of intellectual growth at a global standard. Their influence and impact expanded beyond education, determining moral and political systems and values in society (Gerald, 1927).

As I was getting ready to come to Britain, I also managed to research the history of the reformation, the martyrs of that period and the post-reformation period. These had a huge influence on my decision to come to this country and to serve the people here.

Within six months of my ministry here, some parishioners organised a welcome party at Elizabeth Constantine's house. I dedicated the next two years to getting to know every parishioner and made sure I drove through all the villages and streets where our parishioners lived. This was hugely helpful when called out to minister the sacrament of the sick any time particularly in the middle of the night. Although there were Eucharistic ministers sharing the communion rounds, I too visited the sick and the housebound as often as I could until the start of the COVID-19 pandemic.

Creating a website was important for the Parish's visibility in the area and adding spiritual talks, and new social celebrations like Polish, Filipino and Indian nights brought more people's involvement into the life of the Parish. I started to engage in the local town council and eventually became chaplain to the Mayor Paul Vachon for two consecutive years (2014 & 2015).

Photo by Alan Orr. Fr Darline Presents the book, "Follow me" (Stations of the Cross) written in Poetic style published in 2012 to Cllr Paul Vachon, the Mayor of Okehampton, 2014.

I took the opportunity to write a regular column in a local newspaper on various themes that concern people locally, nationally, and globally. This was vital in enabling me to connect with many people in the area beyond our Catholic population. The invitation from non-Catholics to attend their family functions in their village churches was a heartening experience as these interpersonal relationships are very much part of the Catholic identity.

Our Parish has fewer than 200 parishioners, yet when we had issues getting planning permission for our car park, I experienced the overwhelming support of local people and the town council, with over 1000 signatures in support of our application. Prior to COVID-19 we were pleased to see that most of our social events were attended by a large number of non-Catholics in the area. Over the last 10 years I had the privilege of being present for all but two of these social events amidst my busy academic schedule. The people of the parish were so kind and understanding that they arranged the entire Parish programme around my availability. Unlike any other studies, I knew a true study of psychology is mostly about finding the 'real self', which is in fact an ongoing journey for me. I have experienced parishioners' respect, appreciation, assistance and generosity during that journey.

Blessings

I have always been aware that we would never have been able to do anything well without God's grace and blessing. When it came to pastoral ministry in the Parish, most of the time I found my energy levels high, even after a whole day's academic commitments at the University. My academic achievements and all the successful events we have had in the parish were only possible because of the dedication and generosity of parishioners. I am young enough to be a son or grandson of many parishioners, but I still enjoyed a huge level of respect, trust and support. They have been exceptionally helpful and cooperative. I consider all these as blessings of God, shown to me through my parishioners. In particular I feel it is my honour and duty to make a mention of one person - James Egan, fondly known of as Jim.

➤ Jim Egan

Almost every parishioner who has come into contact with Jim has said how blessed we are to have him in the Parish. His simplicity, dedication, hard work and generosity towards the Parish and to me are those *par excellence* of a true Catholic. None of the work we have undertaken in the Parish has been simple or straightforward. We have been able to build the grotto and the new car park, resurface the area by the house, create a burial area for ashes, replace the rear end of the Church roof, rebuild the collapsed compound wall and repair the ever-leaking chimney in the parish hall. All of these have been complex and needed expert knowledge and management. There were times where we thought we might have to give up pursuing some of the projects, but Jim had the wisdom and patience to find ways to sort out the bottlenecks. He never did anything without my permission and always showed respect for me even though I am young enough to be his grandson. He has been patient with me when I needed explanation and always waited for my approval even though I sometimes had to delay my response. I found him a perfect combination of good character and profound intellect and he has been a wonderful teacher too. My successful study at the British (Exeter, Bristol, Metanoia/Middlesex) Universities and the fruitful and active ministry in this busy Parish would have been impossible without Jim's active involvement and kind benevolence.

Photo by Alan Orr. Grotto & Car park inauguration on 29th April 2018. From the right; Kit Mc Intyre (Jim's sister), Mike Davies, Jim Egan, Jan Goffey (Mayor Okehampton), Melvyn John Stride (MP for Central Devon), Bishop Mark O'Toole, Fr Darline Joseph Marianathan, Hugh Wallace, Canon George Carrick, Canon Peter Morgan, Mgr John Deeny (Vicar General), Mgr George Hay.

I do acknowledge here the dedication and the support offered by many of the other parishioners especially Dr David Rhodes at Chagford and various committees, particularly the Parish Pastoral Committee and the Parish Finance Committee. I have felt on so many occasions I have been blessed by them all.

Aerial view of St Boniface in summer 2015 before the grotto and the car park were built

Aerial view of St Boniface in Spring 2018 after the grotto and the car park were built

Crowning of our Lady underneath the tree in May 2015

Crowning of our Lady in the Grotto May 2019

> *Personal prayer, Therapy and Spiritual Direction*

The one thing I never compromise on in life is the time I give to personal prayers. Prayers have been my life-line. One of the key benefits of being a cradle Catholic with deeply religious parents, is that prayer comes quite spontaneously and naturally. I could feel within me the effect of personal prayer and Mass every day. The body-mind-spirit connection, sense of feeling relaxed and my ability to feel positive are just some of these effects.

I started weekly therapy with Dr Marie Mills since it was mandatory for my Doctoral programme. I hated it in the beginning but eventually started to like it. The whole therapy process with Dr Marie became a powerful help in knowing myself and others well. I have seen many lecturers and professors in my life, both in India and Britain, but none with her intelligence, kindness, generosity and empathy. At times, it felt as if she was sent to save my vocation to the priesthood. Sometimes she was like a mirror reflecting exactly how I felt, especially while I was struggling with emotional vocabulary. She never failed to respect and support my ardent desire to live out my priesthood while continuing my academic commitments., My academic studies obviously mean that I am heavily involved with the secular world. I consider that learning through her has been more important than any other academic challenge and my level of maturity certainly grew during my time in therapy with her. Many colleagues at the University and in the Parish wondered how I have been able to manage my various responsibilities, but Dr. Marie quietly and yet powerfully held me to fulfill my responsibilities to the best of my ability. My weekly therapy sessions were like fueling stations where I was able to refuel sufficiently to keep going until exhausted. She was so generous with her empathy, availability, knowledge and wisdom and I am delighted to say my priesthood was strengthened and enhanced by her therapy sessions.

When I approached Father Kevin Knox-Lecky at the Shrine of Our Lady St Mary of Glastonbury in 2009 asking him to be my spiritual director and confessor, he was hesitant to take me on since I was studying MSc Psychology at Exeter University. After my repeated requests however, he took me on. He was a knowledgeable, caring and wise spiritual director. When I had issues with regard to continuing my life as a priest, he put forward some arguments kindly and wisely, none of which I could sensibly argue with. He was a man of prayer and wisdom. He had a huge influence on me. I found him a strong supporter of my priesthood and he was my spiritual director until he died from a brain tumour, aged 59 at Yeovil District Hospital on 9th October 2014.

After coming to Okehampton Parish, I was looking for a priest similar to Father Kevin. I was pleased to have found Canon David Anear who was the Parish Priest of St Cuthbert Mayne at Launceston at that time. He continues to be my spiritual director and confessor at present. His gentle and caring approach is simple and yet inspirational. He is also a strong supporter of my vocation as a priest.

➢ *Archbishop Mark O' Toole*

There are a good many priests in the diocese who are supportive and appreciative of my study and the ministry in the diocese. Archbishop Mark has been supporting me ever since he became the bishop of this diocese. There were times when he went out of his way to offer me support and help, particularly when I found myself in situations that were too heavy to carry on my own. His letters of appreciation, written to my home archdiocese, are a heartwarming display of how much he values my presence here.

➢ *Archbishop Anthony Anandarayar*

I was fortunate to be a student of Archbishop Anthony Anandarayar at the St. Peter's Pontifical Institute, Bangalore before becoming a priest. As a student of theology, I had already published two books on the Stations of the Cross in English and Tamil. When I approached him to proofread these, he encouraged me to approach the scripture scholars; Rev Dr Lucian Legrand and Rev Dr Aloysius Xavier as they were the leading scholars in those days, and he excused himself with a fair justification that his Doctorate was in Canon law. They were in fact wonderful recommendations with expertise and knowledge not only in scripture but also in English and Tamil languages. After the books were published, I presented them to him, and when he read them, he expressed his happiness with my style of writing which combined spirituality and social concern. I was fortunate to be ordained by him on 26th January 2006 in my own hometown Kolakkudi.

It was the first ordination to have taken place in that village. On that day he released my third book, a Tamil poetry titled, 'Kavidhai.com' co-authored by Fr Kottalam Johnson MSFS.

My relationship with Archbishop Anandarayar was strengthened after I came to Britain, and he was a strong supporter of my ministry here. He encouraged me to continue at Okehampton and Chagford for the good of my priestly vocation. His deep spirituality, simplicity and photographic memory on the matters of Canon Law as well as the books he read were stunning. He had a collection of all my books in Tamil and English and would remember exact sentences and page numbers during our conversations. He was one of those gifted people who are born intelligent. He was very interested in psychology and sometimes, while reading my books, expressed how he missed out learning some basics for a particular subject that he found interesting. He had visited my village Kolakkudi regularly while he was a schoolboy as his uncle's family lived there. 60 years ago, my village was known as one of the very few places in the whole of the Archdiocese for growing rice and fishing. He could remember the names of all seven ponds that surround the village; these are called 'Kolam' in Tamil, hence the village name 'Kolakkudi'. My pen name in Tamil is 'Kolakkudiyar' and Archbishop Anandarayar always took pride in calling me 'Kolakkudiyar' rather than my actual name Darline Joseph.

Every year when I visited him he would say, 'We are priests not for ourselves but for others. How is that going?'

His question made me reflect deeply and became a powerful tool in strengthening my priesthood. He took a personal interest in my growth. Whenever I tried to contact him on his mobile phone, he would always ring back, which he did even a week before he died (on 4th May 2021 aged 75).

We never missed meeting each other when I went home every year on holiday. He was always inspiring and encouraged me to lead a life of priesthood that is simple, authentic and holy. On 4th March 2021 exactly two months before his death, he released updated copies of my books.

Archbishop Anandarayar releases the improved version of my Stations of the Cross in English (on the left) and I present my Neuropsychology self-help book in Tamil (on the right) accompanied by Fr G Maria Anandaraj and Fr R Martin Anthony on 4th March 2021.

Part two of the Neuropsychology self-help book in Tamil is released on 4th March 2021 by the Honorable Minister M C Sambath accompanied by Very Rev Fr R Ratchagar, a well-known veteran Educationist (on the left) and the first copy is given to Dr John Bosco Lourdusamy, a graduate from Oxford University.

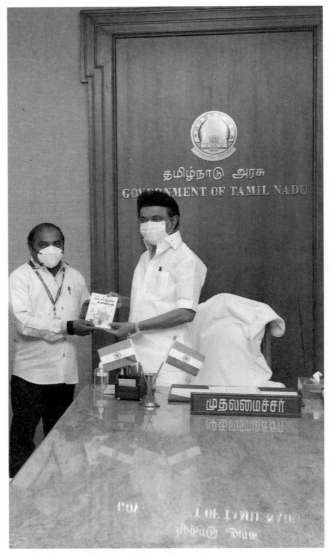

Mr. M.K Stalin, The Honorable Chief Minister of Tamilnadu, India was presented with the part one of my Neuropsychology self-help book in Tamil on 22nd September 2021 by Dr S Peter Anthony Samy, President of Tamilnadu Secretariat Association.

Archbishop of Pondicherry and Cuddalore was presented with my Neuropsychology self-help books in Tamil on 3rd June 2022.

Ma. Subramanian, The Hon'ble Minister for Health, Education and Family Welfare was presented with both of my Neuropsychology self-help book in Tamil on 26th February 2022 by Sr Joyce Roseline, the Principal of St Joseph of Cluny Public School, Neyveli Township, Tamilnadu, India.

C V Ganesan, The Hon'ble Minister for Labour and Employment was presented with both of my Neuropsychology self-help book in Tamil on 26th February 2022 by Sr Joyce Roseline, the Principal of St Joseph of Cluny Public School, Neyveli Township, Tamilnadu, India.

> *Dr Justine Frain*

Almost all my English works have been edited and corrected by Dr Justine Frain. She is a person of deep faith and profound intellect, which is a rare combination. Justine has great insight into my flow of thought and style of communication, which is sometimes not clear for an English audience. She is aware that English isn't my first language as I learned it only late in my teenage years, having missed the opportunity for English study in childhood. Justine hones my writing, and it is fair to say that her generous availability and timely help were crucial to my academic and public writing.

> *Family life*

I feel I am one of the luckiest people in the world to have had very good parents. It is true that they had their own limitations, but they were able to offer the gift of faith to all their children, and especially to me. Nothing in our family happened outside the Church and faith. The entire family took pride in me choosing to become a priest. It was a rather lengthy journey, hard at times but nevertheless, a good one. My vocation promoter Father John Bosco, my uncle Father Antony Samy, Aunty Jovitha Rani and her friend Mrs Jayaseeli Paul Raj have been very much part of that journey as they gave me all the support they could offer. Aunty Jovitha paid for my personal expenses while I was training to be a priest. She also met my ordination costs, which involved the Archbishop coming to my village for the first time. It was an open-air Mass and involved slaughtering 15 goats and 200 chickens to feed 2000 people.

My involvement within the family remained strong, even while I was training to be a priest. It was not always a pleasant feeling to be involved in the inevitable problems faced by my parents, my siblings and their children. But that experience helped me to develop a cohesive sense of self and to be an understanding and a caring pastor in life.

George Bernard Shaw once said, "Parentage is a very important profession, but no test of fitness for it is ever imposed in the interest of the children". Although I have not been a biological parent, I was thrust into a parenting role when I was just 25 years old. I had to care for my nieces and nephews due to an alcoholic brother, as well as the sudden death of my brother-in-law. I found this parenting the hardest thing in the world, whereas by comparison, academic achievement seemed easy. Aiming for perfection in the process of parenting was the most stupid thing I ever did. Looking back, I realise that I learned a lot in my attempt to teach my nieces and nephews.

Children are great imitators and need role models. The proximity of parents and family members makes them automatic role models for children but being a role model is a big task. I call good parents of today 'modern-day martyrs' because, if the children of today are to be raised well, the parenting needs to be built on a virtuous life, with more sacrifice than selfishness; more 'unlearning the old ways' than over-expectation.

Parenting today involves getting the balance right in a world of confusing information about childrearing. There are plenty of parenting manuals, but unfortunately one size does not fit all. I have heard children suffering from too much mother and too little father, or the reverse. They either have too much 'Yes you can' or too much 'No you can't'.

One of the main responsibilities of good parenting is reflective learning. Children of today live in a more complex and challenging world than in the past. Our rapidly changing social and family lives, food habits and techno-logical advances mean that most of our children today grow up so quickly that they can miss a happy and sufficiently lengthy childhood. Therefore, however demanding and challenging it might be, appropriate parenting must match the requirements of today.

Amidst these huge challenges the one thing that every parent is duty bound to do for their children is summed up in the words of Billy Graham: "The greatest legacy one can pass on to one's children and grandchildren is not money or other material things accumulated in one's life, but rather a legacy of character and faith." In spite of my own limitations, through my engagement with my family I think I managed to pass on the legacy of character and faith which I had received from my parents and all those who helped me to become a priest.

> *Dr George Christo & Dr Marie Adams*

These two are very important individuals not only in my academic life but also in my personal life. They both have successful careers in their life on the top of Psychology and psychotherapy. I feel privileged and honored to have had them as my Primary supervisors for my clinical work. I remember the quote from the former president of India, A P J Abdul Kalam who said, "Teaching is a very noble profession that shapes the character, calibre, and future of an individual". It is completely true in my case. They did really help to shape my character. They both are so different in many ways but are similar in their intellectual ability and the offer of genuine empathy which I think have influenced my life greatly.

It was a time when the clergy abuse scandal was storming the press and the public. I did not know if this was playing out in my struggle to find my first clinical placement. Six months after having been assured and reassured of a trainee clinical placement, the offer was withdrawn with a single word, 'sorry' without sensible explanation by the Devon Partnership NHS Trust Exeter. This left me in a very difficult position of not having enough clinical hours to proceed to the third year of my Doctorate. While there was a huge conversation about lack of mental health professionals, I was begging to offer my service freely but no one came forward to take it. I wrote to almost every service in the Exeter and Devon area, but no one would want me. Many services in the area would not even reply to my emails and phone calls. This left me with no hope of finding a placement locally and so I started to look for a placement further away from Exeter. I did go as far as Bristol, but they did not like the fact that I am a Roman Catholic Priest. Many of my peers and teaching staff in Metanoia were sympathetic towards my problem and so suggested that I seek placement in London. I applied to a multi-ethnic counselling service in London run by a person of Indian origin but no luck there either.

I tried couple of NHS services there and got accepted in both of them. I chose to go to Edgeware WDP NHS hospital. Dr George Christo was the Manager of the service there. I found in Dr George a highly intelligent Consultant psychologist, relational counsellor, efficient manager, brilliant supervisor and a caring human being. He holds double Doctorates; one in Clinical Psychology and the other in Research Psychology. He carries an admirable ability to make sense of complicated cases, tailor appropriate

treatments and communicate the same to the members of multi-disci-
plinary team as well as to the trainees in an easily digestible manner which
I think is a rare gift and that is his strength. I experienced his simplicity,
care and understanding that flew naturally indicating his pure genuineness
and noble character in both academic as well as social settings. I liked this
placement under Dr George and learned a lot for my personal life as well
as for clinical world. I stayed there for 18 months. This was the first and
the best of the three placements that I had so far. I used to start at 4 am at
Okehampton and reach Edgware hospital by 9.30 am to see the patients
at 10 am. I used to finish the work by 5.30 pm and then start travelling
back to reach Okehampton by 11 pm the same day. I used to travel to this
placement by car, coach, train and flight. Although I felt knackered until
the following day, yet I enjoyed the learning under Dr George. I had to
end this placement sadly since my Doctorate required placements in three
different settings.

Ending placement with Edgware meant I had to look for a different
Clinical Supervisor and that was what brought me to get in touch with
Dr Marie Adams, although I had a glimpse of her on her farewell party
at Metanoia at the end of my first year. I have stayed with her as super-
visee longer than I was with Dr George. The most important emotional
learning of myself and of my clients happened under her supervision. This
learning was indispensable to get through the essays each year. Dr Marie
Adams having worked for the BBC in a senior position for many years
carries around her the commanding power that gets the work done successfully. She does it so beautifully well without excreting any pressure which
flows out naturally with lots of care, empathy, wisdom and intellect. Dr
Marie's timely help and support have been crucial for my progress academically and personally. Her strong connection with the Catholic faith and
the priesthood made her understand some of my quirky ways and helped
me accordingly with empathy and professionalism. I have experienced her
like a daring Veronica wiping the face of my anxiety and aiding my onward
academic journey. It so happened that I had to come to an abrupt end
with my second clinical placement in the middle of the year in addition
to reeling under the pressure of COVID. Her encouraging supervision

and feedback at that time of massive anxiety held me in one piece. I could feel in Dr Marie a genuine sense of fierce protection and fondness which on reflection I believe to have strengthened my resolve to continue on the course while a few of my peers sadly had to leave over the years.

Study of psychology

My hobby most of the time used to be a passion for learning. I learned various sports such as cricket, volleyball, basketball and ping pong. My undergraduate degrees in philosophy, theology and economics, as well as my postgraduate degree in psychology in India, were not difficult. I loved learning psychology and was interested in the subject even before coming to Britain.

Coming to Britain gave me the opportunity to further my interest in psychology. I managed to complete two psychology postgraduate degrees - an MSc from Exeter University and MEd from Bristol University - and pursue a Doctorate in Counselling Psychology and Psychotherapy (DCPsych) at Metanoia/Middlesex University. The experience of these studies and my clinical work in various settings have shown me the reality of human struggle amid the exquisite goodness, as well as exploitative wickedness, in the world. My resolve to be a better human being and a caring priest has been strengthened through these experiences.

The study of psychology also opened my mind to appreciate and promote the goodness that is present all around us. I had the opportunity to study religious pluralism during my study of philosophy, most of which I researched again later during my psychology degree in Britain. One thing that stood out for me was, "Religion is not only for the religious, but for everyone". There is so much goodness in people. I find many people have an over-emphasis of reasoning, physical experience and experimentation as part of their intellectual endeavour. Their belief is often that anything scientific needs to be upheld while religion is understood as unscientific and needs to be dismissed or ignored.

Science is very important and aids every aspect of our life. However, as humans we still struggle with fear, anxiety, grief, resentment and guilt, for which science on its own has very little to offer. Seeking remedies for these struggles without recourse to religion and its teaching is difficult. Mindset with extreme views of rigidity, dogmatism and authoritarianism, could lead to destructive radicalisation.

There needs to be an integrative approach towards life in order for it to become peaceful, joyful and meaningful. For this reason, there is a need to maintain a balance without resorting to extremes of outright dismissal or unexamined acceptance. There is so much in religion, especially in Christianity, that can make our lives happier and healthier if we can learn the art of finding a balanced and integrative approach. The benefits of religion are not only for those who identify themselves as religious but for everyone, including so-called atheists and agnostics. These ideas were very much at the centre of the reasons why I chose to relate with non-Catholics as well as pursue psychology degrees at the same time while serving our Catholic communities at Okehampton and Chagford.

Challenges

While most of my university companions enjoyed my company and friendship, they could not understand why I was studying for these degrees and as well as continuing to be a priest. Some of the priests too could not understand why I was still in pursuit of psychology studies while running the Parish. It was at times too difficult to explain, but I was pleased that some of the priests in the Plymouth Diocese and most of my parishioners understood the benefit of my learning. There were a few occasions when my learning was put to the test in the Parish.

> ➤ *Death -Emotional vocabulary*

The first three years of my parish ministry involved dealing with an unusually high number of deaths. I anointed most of these people before death and in some cases I was there to pray for them immediately after their death. It felt natural for me to offer empathy with the dying as well as the family of the deceased, however I must confess that it was very difficult at times.

I come from a cultural background that displays in its literature a high level of emotional intensity within relationships. My love for Tamil literature began very early on in my life and my journey into psychology was inspired in my first year of higher secondary school in 1995 during the lessons on Sangam literature (300 BCE to 300 CE). Historically Sangam literature is known as 'the poetry of the nobles' (*Santror cheiyul* in Tamil), and it is the historic evidence of indigenous literary developments in the Tamil language which is found in South India and parallel to Sanskrit. The bulk of the literature forms the basis of Tamil culture and relationship dynamics and has been acknowledged and registered as such by UNESCO (Kumaran, 2007). The vast amount of this literature refers to the poetical exchange of the implicit (*akam* in Tamil) and explicit (*puram* in Tamil) process of feelings and emotions within relationships between individuals and deities. It was written many years before modern psychological researchers examined them. There are many similarities between Sangam literature's implicit poetry and modern understanding of emotional engagements in relationships (Cutler, 1987).

As a Tamil myself, I am passionate about this literature and have engaged in writing and publishing in Tamil from the age of 16. The difficulty I have faced recently has been expressing my feelings and using the correct words of empathy in an English setting. Sometimes, apart from the set prayers, I haven't known what to say to those who were dying. There were times when I just sat listening to the grieving family, saying little and just nodding my head in agreement. It was a struggle within me, but people did not seem to mind as they could sense my empathy through my presence rather than through my words. This became vivid from the cards and letters that people wrote expressing appreciation and gratitude after conducting some of the funerals.

> ## ➢ Change of Mass Time

I was asked to bring forward the Saturday evening Mass from 7pm to 6pm. Most parishioners had voted for this change, but I postponed my decision because two good parishioners, who have been part of the Parish for four decades, were upset about changing the time of what they called 'their Mass'. I could understand their feelings since they had arranged their life around that Mass every Saturday. My invitation to meet in order to explore how this issue could be settled was turned down. I prayed earnestly about how this issue could be addressed without letting down both the parishioners who voted for change as well as the two parishioners who did not want the change. I used every pastoral and psychological tool of diplomacy. After a few weeks they agreed to a meeting in their house, and I spent nearly two hours engaged in conversation with them. At last it sadly ended in vain, as they were adamant that this change was ruthless and unacceptable. I came home feeling frustrated but did not give up, and I continued my prayers for them. After a couple of weeks, they invited me to meet again in their house. I was very pleased that after 30 minutes this time they agreed to the change.

I have found that defenseless and proactive talking, especially when there is opposition to positive change, helps towards deep reflection leading to peaceful resolution. I feel that to be a good shepherd, it is important to learn the art of sensible talking and enduring listening.

It is generally believed that talking is therapeutic. However, it only becomes therapeutic when all parties involved are happy to talk. Healthy talking involves care of oneself as well as the other party. It is about active listening to both the verbal and non-verbal communication, which can be internal as well as external. Healthy talking fosters dialogue, spreads peace and ensures joy. Healthy talking respects difference of opinion and encourages reflective and critical thinking. Healthy talking is natural and spontaneous for people with a secure and safe upbringing, whilst it is difficult and sometimes even impossible for those with a disturbed family background.

Religion has been intertwined with almost every aspect of human life for so long. Christianity, through its seven sacraments (Baptism, Confirmation, Eucharist, Reconciliation, Anointing of the Sick, Matrimony, and Holy Orders), has covered all stages of human existence from birth to death. Learning the Catechism of the Catholic Church can help one lead a healthy life, often reducing, and in some cases alleviating, fear, anxiety, grief, resentment and guilt. When examined with a scientific lens, Christianity can be seen as the religion that offers solutions to deal with terrible human conditions.

Modern minds do sometimes amplify the historical tensions that have existed between science and religion. It is important to be aware of these tensions in order to develop an environment for healthy talking.

Unhealthy talking takes pleasure in aimless chatter and uses the other person as an object. There is neither listening nor observation of communication modes. The person engaging in unhealthy talking finds happiness in spreading rumours, telling lies or speaking behind someone's back. Unhealthy talking is a bad habit, which some people can correct through self-help, while others need therapeutic assistance. The Bible summarises the difference between healthy and unhealthy talking in a powerful way: "The soothing tongue is a tree of life, but a perverse tongue crushes the spirit" (Pro 15:4).

There are seven types of talking therapies in use including CBT (Cognitive Behavioural Therapy) and the more recent EMDR (Eye Movement Desensitisation and Reprocessing) and MBCT (Mindfulness-Based Cognitive Therapy). These therapies are mostly sought due to an occurrence of an unpleasant event. The aim of these therapies is to aid healthy thinking, feeling and behaviour, as well as encouraging healthy talking.

Some people naturally engage in healthy talking while others find they cannot, and the complexities surrounding this have generally been attributed to the formation of character and personality during the later life of a person. Recent neurological research goes far beyond that, revealing how important it is for parents to start healthy talking even to very young babies. Healthy talking among adults, both in the presence of a baby and directly to the baby, helps fire the neurons in the rapidly growing baby's brain which enables it to wire good neurological pathways towards healthy talking later in life. Long before this neuroscience research, St. Paul wrote insightfully to the Ephesians and taught them; "Do not let any unwholesome talk come out of your mouths, but only what is helpful for building others up according to their needs, that it may benefit those who listen" (Eph 4:29).

Our spiritual and social events before COVID-19 involved lots of good talking. When our churches were locked during the pandemic, the Zoom platform was left open at least 20 minutes before and after all the Masses to encourage talking.

Difficulty with a neighbour (The names and dates are omitted in line with the GDPR).

I have been blessed with very good neighbours at Saint Boniface Okehampton. However, the entire parish had difficulty with one particular person due to regular disturbances which included mostly loud music, shouting and yelling.

Offensive and derogatory statements intended to upset our Parishioners regularly appeared on the windscreen of cars next to our Church at St Boniface Okehampton:

Romans go home

Kill the religion and free the people

Stop the Papists

Start war on religion

Bomb the church and build a hospital

These were reported to the police who were aware of the issue, but it went on for some years. Along with many parishioners, I was concerned about this individual and the safety of our parishioners. We had been exploring various possibilities of tackling this situation. I was praying for an amicable solution to ensure the disturbances would stop without causing huge upset to the neighbours and I was also encouraging some parishioners to engage in conversation with him to find out the reasons for his behaviour. I was saddened to hear that he had had a difficult relationship with the Catholic Church in the past and this new knowledge enabled me and most of our parishioners to understand and accept him as he was.

When the time came for him to move, he sent a message to ask if I would go and bless him and his house. Eight parishioners and I went to his house one Friday and I prayed over him and blessed the house. He came to the presbytery later and apologised for all the difficulty he had caused over previous years. His apology melted my heart. At that moment I thought of nothing but the power of prayer in action. I was recalling Jesus's teaching about the call to love everyone, including those who do not love us - or even hate us.

I was also reminded of a Tamil poet, Kaniyan Pungundranar who wrote three thousand years ago, *'Yaadhum oore yaavarum keleer,'* meaning 'All citizens in the universe are our relations and friends'. This insightful statement promotes respect and peaceful cohabitation and shuns discrimination in the face of any possible divisions. The richer meaning of this maxim invites us to deepen our empathic understanding rather than judgmental attitude towards people who behave differently from the rest. This sort of approach can maximise the chance of reconciliation as it happened between us and this person and reduce the harm to all the parties concerned. Most of us have the tendency to respond reactively rather than proactively.

Have we ever stopped to think why we learn 'bad' things quickly while 'good' behaviour takes time and effort. If we want to develop our physique we need to exercise for prolonged periods, but we don't need to do much to develop obesity. Addictions are easy, entertaining and happen quickly but recovery is difficult, draining and slow.

If we want to lead a healthy life, we need to maintain a nutritious diet, but a piece of rotten meat can bring our good health to a standstill within hours. A healthy person can immediately die from the smell of certain poisons, but there is no quick cure that will bring a dying person back to life. We can be quick to lose our temper, but it takes time to calm down. It takes little effort and time to talk nonsense, but real concentration to speak sense.

Why is it that 'bad' is quick while the 'good' takes time. The brain has one system of thinking fast that is instinctive and emotional, while another slow form is more deliberative and logical (Daniel, 2017). Darwin's evolutionary principles of 'survival of the fittest' and 'natural selection' indicate that the most used primary emotions are anger and fear-related (Darwin, 2004). These have dominated humans for many millennia, but through the evolution of civilised society we have fostered other emotions such as happiness, surprise, sadness, embarrassment, guilt and pride. Although anger and fear were instrumental in our early evolution, they are considered somewhat detrimental to our current civilisation. They are, however, quick and easy habits as they have been around so much longer than other emotions. As the saying goes, 'old habits die hard', and it is difficult to change such embedded emotions.

We are still evolving. The speed of each individual's evolution differs according to our own personal and social environments. This needs to be kept in mind when everyone around us does not behave in the way they are expected to. However, we need to concentrate more on deliberative thinking in order to reverse this situation. So that we become quicker at 'good' and slower at 'bad'. Brain plasticity allows lasting change to the brain throughout an individual's life course and shows that our brains are ready, even for structural change, in response to a changing environment. Let us work to create environments that are good, safe, healthy and holy. Even if we don't see the benefits of 'good' coming naturally or quickly, let us at least hope that future generations will reap the fruits of our hard labour. "Do your duty without expecting any reward for your labour." (Chapter 2, Verse 47 – Bhagavad Gita).

My continuing journey

Many in the academic world and the clinical setting keep asking the reasons for my firm desire to continue in my priesthood. The only answer that I keep repeating is, "Priesthood is not a job, it is my way of life, and I will do all that it takes to live joyfully and faithfully". The way I have chosen to take my priestly journey, with the combination of academia and clinical work, is different from many, but I see them as perfectly compatible in helping me to deliver the best to those who believe in God as well as those who do not. I feel able to continue this journey with God's grace and the goodwill of people. I am aware that my ongoing journey is sometimes imperfect. It is regularly nourished by so many good people, but particularly by the question Archbishop Andandarayer asked of me, that I often repeat within myself "We are priests not for ourselves but for others. How that is going?."

Reference

Cutler, N. (1987). *Songs of experience: the poetics of Tamil devotion.* Indiana University Press.

Daniel, K. (2017). Thinking, fast and slow. In.

Darwin, C. (2004). The Descent of Man. 1871. *Reprinted in Penguin Classics Series.*

Davies, G. S. (2008). *Charterhouse in London: Monastery, Mansion, Hospital, School by Gerald S. Davis*: Davies Press.

Gerald Stanley (1927) Monastery, mansion, hospital, school. Charterhouse, London: 1845–1927 26 27 31.

Kumaran, S. (2007). The contribution of Tamil culture to world civilization.

3. Mila[2]: A valiant warrior of faith and death

> "Cowards die many times before their deaths;
> the valiant never taste of death but once."
>
> William Shakespeare

I found Mila valiant in every way. He said he was coming to learn about how to face death peacefully, but halfway through our conversations I realised he was teaching me how to live meaningfully. Hopefully we both had mutual learning and teaching during our meetings.

In the early days of the COVID-19 pandemic, while the general public was still living under the scary and protracted virus, Mila had to shoulder the additional weight of preparing to face an imminent death forced on him by his ill health. I knew I was not an expert in the areas of help he was looking for, and I communicated this to him over the phone when he rang to arrange our first meeting. He acknowledged I was not an expert, but he was convinced that I could be an active listener who could help him discover the available resources within himself. Mila did eventually become an expert in handling his anxiety and fear. His physical being was becoming weak, but his spirit was emerging strongly. It was clear from our meetings that he was prepared to embrace death bravely when it arrived. He was able to do it with the support of his Catholic faith, his beloved wife Paula, his loving children Jon, Rob, and Will, family members, and many good people in the cancer charity Force.

Meeting on Sunday 18th October 2020

It was a short meeting, lasting only 20 minutes, but it contained everything that would put me in reflective mode for the rest of the week. This meeting was not pre-arranged, so we did not sit down for a proper conversation. In fact, Mila approached me after Mass to arrange a meeting,

---

2   All the names in this chapter are anonymised at the request of the family members.

but we ended up talking in front of Our Lady's grotto for the next 20 minutes.

As usual Mila greeted me with his spontaneous and relaxed smile. I reciprocated, along with a caring enquiry about his beloved son Will's unusual absence from Church that day. Mila said he had heard about the rapid mutation and fast spread of the COVID 19 Virus and decided to leave Will at home rather than take any risk. Mila then asked about my availability for a proper chat during the week. While I was giving him a few dates and times from memory, I noticed tears rolling down his cheeks. I realised that something was not right and persuaded him to tell me what was happening. He managed to smile despite the tears and I recalled a saying by Whitney Fancher that I had read a while ago:

"Tears are words
The heart can't express."

I suggested a couple of dates and times when we could meet during the following week and he started to sob like a child. This broke my heart and I asked him if he would like to sit on the bench in front of the grotto.

He controlled his tears and said, "Father, I wanted to touch base with you in case I lose the ability to speak in the coming weeks". When I heard this, I guessed there was something serious going on and agreed to offer him the space he needed.

We sat on the bench and he started to describe his health condition to me. He seemed calm and serene when he talked about the seriousness of his health, and yet he expressed hope of seeing a light at the end of the dark tunnel. However, his tears continued and I felt the struggle between the reality of his health condition and the hope of recovery he envisioned. I noticed my tears too as I listened to Mila and I felt anxious and angry at the restless dialogue that was going on within me. I was struggling to find words to comfort him beyond just mirroring his feelings and being there for him. I knew I was unprepared and didn't want to be dismissive, but at the same time I didn't know how to handle such an emotionally charged space. In addition, I was angry and questioning why this had to happen to a good man like Mila. I have known some very nice people including my own fantastic spiritual director Father Kevin Knox Lecky who used to be the Parish Priest at Glastonbury, died prematurely due to sudden ill health. While dealing with my own discomfort and anger, I just managed to stay attuned to Mila's feelings of desperation and helplessness.

We decided to resume our conversation later that day over the phone, but then postponed it since Mila's children were at home and he did not want them to notice how he was struggling.

I was wondering if I had handled the situation sensibly or meaningfully enough. Did he get anything at all out of our unplanned meeting? A couple of days later, Mila spotted me in our car park during my usual rosary walk. While part of me wanted to find out how he felt after our meeting last Sunday, I also wanted to ask how he was coping. He may have sensed my feelings as he spoke about how powerful our chat on Sunday had been. He said he had truly found comfort and strength from our meeting and continued by saying that I represented everything about empathy that he had read. He recalled a saying that I found very powerful and wrote down as soon as I came back to the presbytery:

"Empathy is
Seeing with the eyes of another,
Listening with the ears of another,
Understanding with the brain of another,
And feeling with the heart of another."

I started to reflect on what he said. Although I knew that I tried my best to be there for him, I did not know how I had been able to achieve this, since our encounter was unplanned and I was totally unprepared. However, I knew that being in the presence of Our Lady in front of the grotto was empowering. As a devotee of the Blessed Mother Mary, I believe I had been given the inspiration to offer him what he had needed, even though I had found it difficult to express. Although I had connected with him on an emotional level, the feeling of inadequacy on an intellectual level left me rather confused. First of all, I did not know the correct words to use that could sooth his helplessness, and secondly, I was uncertain of what I could offer that would match his needs and expectations.

I remembered some of the skills that had been taught during my training both as a Priest and a Psychologist that would help me to respond to a complex reality such as Mila's, but I realised that our meeting required the presence of my authentic self rather than my skills. Mila had a peaceful and warm presence and a calm voice, which were part of his personality and seemed to flow naturally from and through him. I guess these helped him to draw the empathy I had for him, although I was struggling to verbalise it. This experience left me with the conviction that there is nothing as powerful as the authentic self when it comes to comforting a person in distress as opposed to any powerful academic tool. We were drawn to each other's authentic selves and could feel comfortable with our vulnerabilities without any fear of being judged. Parishioners who know me well have often asked how I am able to connect with people so spontaneously, given my collectivist cultural background, where expressing emotions by men are discouraged. Emotional expression is usually seen more as a weakness than a strength. I must confess that I am still struggling and learning but my answer to that is twofold: my learning comes from both historical and personal experiences.

On a historical level, I am a Tamil speaking Indian. My primary and secondary education were both in Tamil and I love the Tamil language so much that I started to write for publication in Tamil at the age of 16. Tamil is one of the classical languages with rich literature. I was particularly interested in the *Sangam literature* known as 'The poetry of the nobles' (*Santror cheiyul* in Tamil) dating back to 300 BCE to 300 CE. This literature is the historic evidence of indigenous literary developments in the Tamil language found in South India parallel to Sanskrit. The bulk of the literature forms the basis of the Tamil culture and the relationship dynamics. This has been acknowledged and registered by UNESCO (Kumaran, 2007). The vast amount of this literature refers to a poetical exchange of implicit (*akam* in Tamil) and explicit (*puram* in Tamil) process of feelings and emotions in relationships between individuals and deities, a long time before the modern psychological researchers came to explore them. There are lots of similarities and parallels between Sangam literature's implicit poetry and the modern discovery of emotional engagements in relationships (Cutler, 1987).

On a personal level, I feel fortunate to have been exposed to the best of these two worlds: the study of Sangam literature in Tamilnadu, India in my earlier days and my study and research in psychology now in Britain. However, as a Tamil myself, although it is not too difficult to connect on emotional level, the challenge lies in verbalising the same in the English language and its unique cultural setting.

Meeting on 21st October 2020

We arranged this meeting through our email communication. Prior to our meeting I had referred myself to some pastoral guidance and psycho-therapeutic techniques to help me deal with Mila's unique situation. They gave me a huge amount of confidence in the initial stages of our conversation, but halfway through our meeting, I realised that Mila needed more of my authentic self to be there to listen to him than offer him tools to cope with his difficulty. With this in mind I decided to be there for Mila rather than setting my own agenda.

Mila spoke quietly yet steadily and firmly. I thought he may have *thanatophobia* which is a form of anxiety that a person has about the fear of one's own death or the process of dying. It is commonly referred to as *death anxiety*. Mila did have traces of that but seemed to manage it amazingly well with his power of positive thinking. His positive thinking was not based on irrational belief or blind faith but on realism and courage. He was able to steer around the difficult terrain of his health condition. While doing so, he was able to articulate his own medical diagnosis as well as procedures and treatments whilst having the incredible awareness of his slim chance of survival at the end. To my surprise, he did not seem to display overtly any immediate anxiety such as hot flushes, sweating, avoidance or complacency. His amazing sense of grace and serenity kept our conversation going. Although I was not talking much, Mila knew I was there for him,

engaged in his process of making sense of his situation. He was able to articulate his emotions in a contained and balanced way. I found this incredible
and felt as if I was being prepared pastorally as a priest to face encounters of
this sort in the future comfortably.

In total we met five times and exchanged a number of emails before he
sadly passed away on 11th April 2021 aged 58. Although he lived just a
short distance from the presbytery, I could not go out as I had to isolate
having just travelled back from India where I had gone to participate in the
first anniversary of my father's death. I did have the opportunity to pray
over Mila via the phone and felt an intense sorrow dawning on me; all our
meetings ended with praying together and this time I was praying over him
on my own.

> "Death leaves a heartache no one can heal,
>
> love leaves a memory no one can steal."
>
> From an Irish headstone.

Our meetings were so powerful in every way. For Mila, his health issues
and the imminent death appeared less important when compared to the
wellbeing of his wife and children. He was more concerned about his
families' pain of losing him than his own fear of death. He valued his family
very much and he spoke at length how much they meant for him. We got
involved echoing each other's' views about family since I too consider
family as a blessing and advocate the importance of family life and family
formation in both my writing and speaking.

I remember some time ago there was an article in the local newspaper
about the need for 7,600 more families nationwide this year to offer homes
to the rising number of children referred for care. Some of the couples were
interviewed on how they felt fostering a child. Their response was more of a
joy in caring as a family than a challenging burden. From my conversations
with Mila, I was convinced that he was truly a family man and loved his
family above everything else. He celebrated the big and small successes of
his children.

Pumpkin carving for Halloween 2020 by Will, Mila's eldest son

All our meetings started and ended with prayers. Mila's care for his family, his ability to hold himself intact while making sense of his health and death, his modest participation in our parish events and the regular Mass attendance with Will were fine indicators of his rock solid Catholic faith. Mila expressed gratefulness on several occasions for the gift of faith. He had a special love for the Catholic Church.

Writing the history and development of human survival and civilisation would be incomplete without significant reference to religions. Every true religion unmistakably illustrates the depth of ardent enthusiasm for peace, perfection and joy for the entire human race. But sadly, some religions at some point in history were faced with fierce wars and violence – and some against each other. Christianity also is not an exemption to this primordial phenomenon. However, it does have an unquestionably elevated place in history, with its secular and sacred doctrines and rituals which deal with humans' natural journey from cradle to grave. Having been an integral part of the human race from the very beginning, Christianity undoubtedly has been more of 'a way of life' than like any other religion.

Living and practising Christianity has had mixed consequences in history. Most of them were largely constructive while some were badly destructive. Yet, it is one of the very few religions in the world that has geared up successfully to address humans' social, economic and political concerns by following the powerful teaching of Jesus's command to 'love one another; just as I have loved you' (John 13:34). So far, this maxim has been the rule of law in every civilised society, be it Christian or not.

There is no running away from the fact that there have been tensions between what Christianity claimed to be true and what science has established. Reports of abuse of power and authority has, in the past, brought Christianity to its knees. Nonetheless, Christianity had the courage to 'put its house in order'. It must be remembered that mistakes have been acknowledged, apologies have been made and lessons have been learned. Progress has been outstanding due to the fact that Christianity is adaptive and engages with the world more widely than ever before. This is because there is an increased awareness of the truth that God isn't 'up there somewhere' but down here with us, sharing our daily joys and sorrows. I knew from my conversations with Mila that he was very much aware of this reality.

The poignant encounters with Mila were extremely powerful. They left me with a sense of humility and a longing to look out for different ways in which God communicates. My desire to be a good shepherd got strengthened through my experience with Mila.

Reference

Cutler, N. (1987). *Songs of experience: the poetics of Tamil devotion.* Indiana University Press.

Kumaran, S. (2007). The contribution of Tamil culture to world civilization.

4. Mayda Gertrude Reynolds's simple and yet exemplary faith

In 2018 after the month-long preparation in the lead-up to Christmas I thought I could rest for few days, but on 26th December I decided to drive the 120 miles to Salisbury hospital to visit Mayda. The nearer I drew, the lesser was my feeling of tiredness and I noticed more mixed emotions of joy and sadness within myself.

The feeling of joy was intensely associated with my clear memory of how Mayda carried her faith throughout her life and expressed it so tangibly to people like me. I would not have survived happily as a priest for so long in Okehampton & Chagford if it were it not for people like Mayda who made my heart full of joy, lightened my burdens and brightened my priesthood. I see Mayda's life as a good reflection of the fantastic quotation by the Indian poet Rabindranath Tagore:

> "I slept and dreamt that life was joy.
>
> I awoke and saw that life was service.
>
> I acted and behold, service was joy."

Mayda's faith inspired her to understand life as joy and service, ultimately seeing 'service as joy' throughout her life. She had the charisma to transfer this to her children, grandchildren and others like me. I had the privilege of experiencing this and being inspired by her in Chagford and at her home in Jersey.

As I neared Salisbury hospital, I noticed that the anticipated joy of seeing her had diffused my sense of tiredness, but I had an intense feeling of sadness too since it would be my last visit to Mayda as she neared inevitable death. However, I managed to hold my emotions together and concentrate on driving.

As Mayda lay in hospital surrounded by her grandchildren David, Ellie, Joanna and Karina, her daughter Mary and son-in-law Anthony, the experience was special in every way. Mayda remained quiet, her eyes closed and her body still, but I knew she recognised my presence. Our shared language for the first few seconds was silence, but a silence that had a profound communication between all of us standing around her bed. The simmering emotions of our shared silence were probably similar, since Mayda had impacted all our lives on a personal level. I could sense the desire to hold the shared emotion of sadness with the power of prayer, so I began the prayer for the dying and then anointed her. Mayda knew we were all there praying for her.

The routine reality of a priest's life is being called out for emergency pastoral duty at any time, often in the middle of the night or very early in the morning. During the 10 years that I have been living and serving in this area, I have conducted more funerals than christenings and weddings. I have been fortunate enough to anoint most of the dying before death and have been with many immediately after death. In some cases, I was able to be there even before the doctors or emergency crew arrived. Among many similar patterns of behaviours, the one that stands out for me is the determination of the sick person to hold on until prayers and anointing have been conducted for them. Mayda did hold on for me to visit her until after Christmas although doctors had predicted her death earlier.

It was as if Mayda's faith helped her defy the medical prediction and kept her safe until I arrived and prayed over her. I knew she had had a heart attack in 2016 and her consultant gave her a life expectancy of just two years. She did not dwell on it, but trusted in God's providence that she would go whenever she was called. I saw how Mayda's family members were surprised by the way she responded to the prayers and the anointing. I thought it was a powerful witness to all of us as well as the people in the hospital.

My faith was strengthened after I went to study neuroscience at Bristol University. Looking at the response from Mayda I was aware of the explanations that scientific studies have revealed. Some of the research on 'end of life' and 'near death experience' confirm that brain-mind functions are very different in those who have religious faith compared to those who do not (Marrone, 1999). The neuro-imaging investigations reveal that prayer triggers certain types of brain activation and stimulation, even though all other parts of the body remain immobile while waiting to die. The part of the temporal lobe that some researchers call the 'God-Spot' is involved in complex and multidimensional activity and has been evolving in humans for many millennia. It heavily influences the general developmental stages of humans, including cognitive processes, emotional and personality development. This simply means we are naturally disposed to be 'God seekers', whether one holds faith in God or not, and explains why dying people hold on until prayers and anointing are administered (Schmidt, 2008).

These ideas of 'God spot' and 'God seekers' are better explained through the physical and mental health outcomes that prayer brings to people. In the last decade the neglected subject of how prayer/faith/spirituality can heal has been put under rigorous scientific examination by researchers throughout the world. I was personally interested in the subject 'brain, mind and behaviour' during my MEd degree at Bristol University. There are studies that confirm the implications of spiritual experiences on healing through the neurofunctionality of brain-mind relationship (Bennett et al., 2007).

Some extraordinary spiritual experiences, for which explanations are very scarce were once considered a consequence of psychological or brain disorders. Recently however, neurofunctional studies on spiritual experiences reveal how several brain areas get activated producing complex function patterns that have health benefits (Moreira-Almeida, 2013).

In the case of Christian prayer, the specific part of the brain, the 'God spot' in the temporal lobe, is in active stimulation causing multidimensional functions (evoking positive emotions such as love, hope, forgiveness and contentment) in human behaviour and relationship. These have an impact on the neural pathways which connect the endocrine and immune systems. Therefore, prayer causing spiritual experience reduces arousal in the SNS (sympathetic nervous system) and HPA (hypothalamic-pituitary-adrenal axis) restoring physiological stability and strengthening immune capability. More specifically this process enhances cardiovascular muscles and boosts positive mood with self-esteem (Hughes, 1997).

There is much debate among multi-discipline experts as to how we can best look after ourselves. The unanimous view is to create a model of care focused on physiological and psychological wellbeing. This has resulted in the formation of the latest 'bio-psychosocial-spiritual' model of health care that provides the framework for integrating one's religious faith into clinical practice (Besemann et al., 2018).

I thought the extraordinary response of Mayda's faith was an open invitation to all of us to enter into deep reflection within ourselves. If we would like to build a healthy society, along with our best medical professionals we need to have prayer habits just like Mayda had. Through her prayer life, she had a huge influence on her children and grandchildren. I think it is worth presenting here what they all had said about the impact of Mayda's prayer life on them.

Granny had little prayer cards in various places including her bedside table.

Granny regularly prayed the Rosary. Granny embraced technology and used the Laudate App every morning before breakfast for the Daily Readings and was always interested in Saint of the Day.

Granny's spirituality was probably responsible for her ability to stay calm, thoughtful and loving regardless of events around her. Granny instilled such confidence in us that God made us who we are. He is proud of us and that we should not wish to change anything about ourselves.

Granny was someone so loyal to God, so kind and so loving, we always trusted that God would listen particularly carefully to granny's prayers.... if granny helped us pray or prayed for us, it strengthened our faith that God's will would be done.

Granny established family prayer time. The prayer "Lord keep us safe this night" has been passed through the generations to the great grandchildren.

Granny encouraged us to pray to saints like St. Anthony if something was lost.

Granny's spirituality was inseparable from her outlook on life, which was without exception always positive.

Granny made every effort to go to church. Despite on several occasions fainting in church, this did not deter her.

Everyone in the Binns family carries the good vibration of Mayda, the reflection of her faith shining through the love of family life. I know this is what connected me so quickly with the family. I've attended three world-class universities in Britain and served in Okehampton and Chagford for the last 10 years so I've made lots of friends, but there is something special about the Binns family. I have experienced all the healthy aspects of life in my relationship with them: faith, kindness, generosity, care, food, friendship - and their family competitiveness in basketball and table tennis! The family was able to offer these spontaneously just because they were a good family and my relationship with them has been crucial in strengthening my priesthood and personal wellbeing.

Having a good family is a blessing. Faith and religion as in the case of Mayda provide lots of opportunities to have and harbour a good family. I recall an article in The Times about the nationwide need for 7,600 more families in UK to offer homes to the rising number of children referred for care. Almost every family interviewed in that article spoke about how fostering a child was the noblest task and all cited more joy than challenges in their caring and sharing as a family.

As Princess Diana once so intuitively said, "Family is the most important thing in the world". It is indeed so. As a society, our benevolent urge to care for deserving children has led us to try various methods of care: orphanages, children's homes, youth treatment centres and rehabilitation homes, mostly run by religious groups and charities. These provide housing, education and care of the children, but none can serve as well as a family. I think this is the reason for Fostering Foundation UK's plea for more foster families.

A good family is a place of blessing where love flows naturally and unconditionally. It is where we begin to live and learn how to face success and failure. A healthy family offers solid emotional and relationship support and security. It is a place of peace and joy, providing not only the important social fabric, but also everything that helps a child develop as a healthy individual, as a valuable member of a community and as a conscientious member of a civilised nation. A good family is a launch pad that supports the development of good personality and positive change.

According to research by Global Development Organization, the UK has the highest rate of family breakdown in the western world. This results in huge economic, social and emotional cost, and relationship misery.

A report issued by the Centre for Social Justice states: "...the overriding priority of family policy...is best summed up in one statistic, 48% of all children born today will see the breakdown of their parents' relationship". The disruption of family breakdown reflects on the wellbeing of the children in these families. This must change if we are to protect children. Most of the problems in the family can be solved if we try to follow what St. Paul said: 'Bear with each other and forgive one another if any of you has a grievance against someone. Forgive as the Lord forgave you.' (Colossians 3:13).

It was a heart-breaking experience to leave the hospital and Mayda after the prayers, since I knew there was no possibility of seeing her again. She passed away on 2nd January 2019, six days after my visit.

I experienced the impact of Mayda's deep faith shining through her warm presence in the hospital as well as on several other occasions, particularly in Jersey in 2014 when I went for her granddaughter Joanna's wedding to Richard. I was the main celebrant of the wedding Mass. All my time in Jersey, before, during and after the wedding, I found her to be a person with a deep message for me, a message that would define my convictions about life. I felt her graceful presence and her gentle, empowering smile. There was an aura of tranquillity surrounding her. I have read in the past about the power of presence but that was my first opportunity to experience it. Since it was a wedding trip, there were busy and joyous noises around. I found Mayda 'being there'- acknowledging, appreciating and encouraging everyone's involvement in whatever was going on. After that experience, I became aware of how important it is to 'be there'. I have tried as a psychologist as well as a priest to 'be there' but it is a challenging task.

Actively being with someone involves listening with care. It can be a draining exercise, especially if it involves multiple emotional engagements and responses. We experience huge fluctuations of emotions when people around us are sharing their thoughts and concerns. At the Parish fair I recall hearing from people: "It's marvellous and wonderful that my daughter just had a lovely baby girl after being desperate for years": "I am still grief-stricken and devastated because my friend, who is only 40 years old, died last week": "I am terribly scared and nervous as I am going to hospital tomorrow for a scan": "I am so happy and relieved that I have been given clearance by my consultant of a dreadful sickness that has dogged me for a decade": "I am looking forward to going on holiday next week": "We are so pleased that our son is graduating in January".

Such scenarios lead to feelings of happiness and sadness in varying degrees and generate appropriate emotional responses. It's tiring yet rewarding. It's challenging yet overwhelming. We all need somebody for actively 'being' and listening with care. These are the simple ingredients of our daily life, bringing joy alongside the usual challenges and troubles. They help us guard against psychological distress and potential meltdown into mental health problems.

Jesus went a step further by loving and doing. It is hard to live like Jesus, but I think people like Mayda have tried and have shown us the way so that we can also try. Even if it is not possible to live as exactly as Jesus, at least to some extent we can follow some of his preaching as we see in the words of St. Paul: "Be kind to one another, tender hearted, forgiving one another as God in Christ forgave you". (Ephesians 4:32).

We are very good at enjoying the positive perks of life such as good health, successful relationships, economic success, parties and nice dinners. Nevertheless, when it comes to coping with ill health, sickness, failures and poverty, most of us struggle and some of us can never cope. Life for those becomes a misery. They find nothing to look forward to in life. The very thought of baby Jesus in the manger surrounded by angels, Mary, Joseph, animals and shepherds invites us to reflect on the complexity of life's reality and yet to live in joy and happiness. The good news from the angel to Mary and Joseph was received with both joy and anxiety. The birth in the manger was both a relief and discomfort. Giving birth in the night amidst livestock would have been harmless and yet scary.

"Life is 10% what happens to you and 90% how you react to it" said Charles R. Swindoll. Mary and Joseph reacted joyfully and offer the same to us all, despite the challenges and hardships. I think Mayda tried to follow that example in her life of being a devout Catholic, continuing joyfully amidst challenging realities.

Driving home from Salisbury hospital to Okehampton was a difficult journey with heavy traffic, but my mind was active with Mayda's memory and filled with mixed emotions. Therefore I didn't feel tired. The spiritual part of me was reassured that she would soon be with the Lord and free from the aches and pains of this earthly world, but the human part of me was struggling to cope with the fast-approaching loss. I was trying to self-soothe by recalling the reflection I had given on the theme 'hope in life' during my anointing. Mayda's life of faith was marked with hope in the Lord.

It is hope that lets people like Mayda draw inspiration from the risen Jesus despite the challenges and difficulties that are faced in life. There could be no better example than Jesus for the life-saving virtue of hope. His hope was both spiritual and scientific. Jesus showed his spirituality in the way he employed his sense of foresight and wisdom to deal with what was coming, and how he must address that. Prayer and meditation were the means that connected his spirituality with God the Father. That gave him positive energy to understand, assess and act on unfolding events. As I read through the eulogy notes from Mayda's son Mike, I understood how she emulated Jesus in every walk of her life. Her faith was active and present in everything she did. Whether it was engaging with family, friends, the natural environment, gardens or wildlife, she had a natural ability to inspire and change.

This natural drive was at work when she took responsibility for her garden at Westward, which she tended for almost forty years. It was destroyed by the great storm of October 1987, but Mayda was determined to rebuild it before the following summer for tourists to enjoy her garden. Her love of the garden and interest in camellias connected her with the International Camellia Society and she became the society's president in the mid-1990s, travelling extensively with the society for four decades. Mayda collected over two hundred varieties of camellias and had varieties in bloom over nine months of the year. Camellias have an interesting Catholic connection. The genus was named by Linnaeus after the Jesuit botanist George Joseph Kamel (1661-1706), a Catholic missionary in the Philippines who had an interest in botany, pharmacy and nature and intro-duced Philippine flora and fauna to Europe (Cullum, 1956).

I imagine that Mayda was able to smell the "Catholic" fragrance of camellias and share their aroma with everyone around her. It is clear that Mayda had an immense power to effect change for better, another aspect of her following the example of Jesus. His teachings were realistically powerful and charged with an immense capacity to change thoughts, feelings and behaviours. Modern clinical psychology has set out means to scientifically and clinically measure this. Jesus' preaching made a deep impression on people's lives so that they could effect change in themselves. His teaching of "Love one another as I have loved you" was a radical departure from the Old Testament teaching of "an eye for an eye and a tooth for a tooth". His healing miracles, accompanied with words and actions, had a direct effect on people. His ability to forgive even at the point of death on the cross, was the supreme example of a selfless carer verses selfish humanity. His hope was spiritual and scientific, but it was not free from test. His agony in the Garden of Gethsemane and His temptation by the devil, show that even Jesus had to undergo tests of hope.

Most of us have hope, and some of us succumb to the tests of hope. One such modern day test is the marked tension between science and spirituality. These are sometimes presented as opposites that cause conflict and loss of hope. But they can co-exist perfectly and promote harmony. It is clear that Mayda had a natural ability to hold these perceived opposites and create hope instead of conflict. It was her faith that gave her hope and empowered her to face life as it is with all its joys and sorrows – and pass that on to people like me.

I believe Mayda's strong faith helped her face the reality of life. I don't remember a time she appeared without a smile. She had a smiling face even on her deathbed. It is important to keep smiling. Many research studies that have investigated the benefit of smiling state that it brings an increase in overall lifespan. They have proven scientifically the philosophy of the smiling Buddha - smiling makes us feel relaxed, elevates mood, relieves stress, reduces pain, lowers blood pressure, and increases immunity contributing to an ability to stay calm and be positive even in adverse situations (Neuhoff & Schaefer, 2002).

I think the following statement summarises the life of Mayda with a powerful message.

"It is not death that a man should fear,
but he should fear never beginning to live."

Marcus Aurelius

Reference

Bennett, M. R., Dennett, D., Dennett, D. C., Hacker, P., & Searle, J. (2007). *Neuroscience and philosophy: Brain, mind, and language.* Columbia University Press.

Besemann, L. M., Hebert, J., Thompson, J. M., Cooper, R. A., Gupta, G., Brémault-Phillips, S., & Dentry, S. J. (2018). Reflections on recovery, rehabilitation and reintegration of injured service members and veterans from a bio-psychosocial-spiritual perspective. *Canadian Journal of Surgery, 61*(6 Suppl 1), S219.

Cullum, L. A. (1956). Georg Joseph Kamel: Philippine botanist, physician, pharmacist. *Philippine studies, 4*(2), 319-339.

Hughes, C. E. (1997). Prayer and healing: A case study. *Journal of Holistic Nursing, 15*(3), 318-324.

Marrone, R. (1999). Dying, mourning, and spirituality: A psychological perspective. *Death studies, 23*(6), 495-519.

Moreira-Almeida, A. (2013). Scientific research on mediumship and mind-brain relationship: reviewing the evidence. *Revista De Psiquiatria Clinica, 40*(6), 233-240.

Neuhoff, C. C., & Schaefer, C. (2002). Effects of laughing, smiling, and howling on mood. *Psychological reports, 91*(3_suppl), 1079-1080.

Schmidt, R. H. (2008). *God seekers: Twenty centuries of Christian spiritualities.* Wm. B. Eerdmans Publishing.

5. Jean Nyburg's heart-warming contribution

It is said that there are two greatly significant days in a Catholic priest's life. The first of these is the day of his ordination and the second is the day he discovers his purpose as a priest. For me personally, the joy that overwhelmed me on the day I explored the purpose of my priesthood was far greater than the day I was ordained a priest.

I discovered the true purpose of my priesthood at around 2 pm on Friday 17th August 2018 while I was ministering the Sacrament of the Sick to an elderly parishioner called Jean Nyburg. I have never felt so emotionally moved and confused as I did on that day. It was one of the most poignant moments of my life, even though I had already been a priest for the past 12 years. While I watched Jean getting ready to fade away from this painful world into a peaceful paradise, I had a sense of relief but was equally charged with a force of sadness at the permanent loss of her presence. As I opened my oil stock and prayer book to anoint her, I felt grief-stricken and unusually nervous. The prayer book began to shake in my hands, tears started to wet my cheeks and I shook like a child, sobbing uncontrollably. There were two people standing with me - Jean's daughter Sue and the manager of the care home, Margaret Haxton - and I felt rather awkward at the thought of what they would think of me, a priest weeping and fumbling with his books while undertaking this important and solemn ministry.

Contrary to my thinking, Margaret Haxton, who is one of our devout parishioners, came over and put her arms around my shoulders, gently empathising with me. With the help of her reassuring presence, I completed the prayer of anointing, which didn't take long, but afterwards I felt too uncomfortable to stay and chat. That is very unusual for a person like me who naturally falls into conversation, especially in such a sombre situation. I tried to force myself to stay but could not resist my inner urge to quit the room. It was a very strange feeling and on reflection, I realised I had never felt that before. I can remember in detail how, irrespective of whether it was a day or a night, I have anchored myself whenever and wherever I found people affected by grief or loss, offering my empathy and sympathy for hours in some stressful and difficult situations. Contrary to my usual routine, on this occasion I excused myself and departed the scene as quickly as I could.

Driving back home was not easy as feelings of sadness and grief overwhelmed me. Fond memories of Jean were crowding my mind, convincing me that she was going to be with the Lord and there was neither a need for excessive emotional upheaval nor undue worry. However, I could not stop the normal empathetic human feelings of someone whose priestly life and vocation had been enriched by a person such as Jean.

Jean was a great soul with an enormous amount of love, respect and care for the parish and her priests. Although she called me a 'special priest', I was informed she had been just as fond of most of the priests at Holy Family Church. She was the last of a small group of women who in 1957 began to raise the necessary funds to build the Holy Family church at Chagford. Only two other long-standing parishioners, Mary Sheridan and Alice Wells, remember the first mass in 1963.

When I moved into the parish in 2011, Jean engineered the idea of a welcome party in Elizabeth Constantine's house. To my surprise almost the entire Holy Family, Chagford congregation was present for a sumptuous lunch, welcoming me with a warmth which I felt instantly.

I hold the parishioners of Holy Family Chagford very close to my heart, not only because they welcomed me in this way, but also for enriching my priesthood in so many ways. Although I was enthusiastic with my ministry to the people outwardly, I was struggling inwardly, questioning whether I should continue my priesthood, since my world of academia was promising me a lot of other options. In the words of one of my research colleagues, a 'bright future was ahead of me' if I left my priesthood and joined his team. Although my head was crowded with questions of 'ifs' and 'buts', the people of Chagford captured my heart. Jean used to say to me: "You go wherever you want and study whatever you need to, but please do not leave us". People both in Okehampton and Chagford were really caring in helping me to live my priesthood in full. Some of the parishioners were very generous in offering me non-judgmental support that was packed with genuine love and care. There were plenty of invitations for wining and dining, opportunities for trying my skills at shooting or riding, or to enjoy my favourite competitive sports of table-tennis and basketball. Within a couple of years of my arrival in the parish, I began to feel settled due to the care, concern and love of the parishioners who supported my overall wellbeing. Jean certainly was one of the parishioners who most enriched my priesthood and helped me to get grounded in the parish.

At the house of Elizabeth Constantine on Thursday 7th June 2012

Jean would never finalise the hymns she chose for Sunday Mass unless they had been agreed by me on the previous Thursday before the Mass. She was a regular attendee at Masses on Thursdays and Sundays until early 2017 when, as her mobility was restricted, she chose to watch the Mass through Skype. She would then give me honest comments about my homilies through emails and phone calls!

Jean appeared unassuming yet she was very clever and had an incredible memory, even in her 90s. She had an admirable humility and yet was proud of Britain. People who knew her well will know of her past career in Bletchley Park where she is commemorated on the codebreakers wall, yet she never uttered a word about it to me.

Jean Nyburg's name on codebreakers wall at Bletchley Park

Whenever I visited her at home, initially in her flat and later on at the care home, we spoke at length on various topics. She used to say how bad the Second World War was, but that it had changed Britain for the better for everyone. She said that just like the war, so had colonisation changed the world for the better, in spite of the exploitation, war and violence. I was rather perplexed by that statement, as it was a totally new perspective on what I had been taught back in India. I wanted to check if Jean was telling me the truth. To my surprise and horror, I discovered that the heinous social practises of many public evils were eradicated in India during the British Raj. These included 'sati' where a wife was thrown into the same funeral pyre as her dead husband, and 'untouchability' where the lower castes were never to be seen or touched by the higher castes. Last year while I was completing a Tamil book on neuropsychology, I came across some of the audio tapes of Periyar E.V. Ramasay (1879-1973), a Tamil-Indian social activist who made a public plea to the British during

Indian independence, that they should not abandon the Indians to the higher castes but continue to rule, even if they had to do so from Britain. It was after that conversation with Jean that I started to research more about colonisation and its impact, both good and bad. Before the British Raj, the caste system justified by Indian religions was a death trap which glorified the higher castes and dehumanised the lower castes. The lower castes were treated as untouchables; they were not allowed to enter places of worship, nor were they allowed to wear sandals and neither men nor women were allowed to cover their upper bodies. Education was the preserve of the higher castes. The British Raj passed legislation to prevent all of these and similar social evils, although the complete eradication of the caste system was not possible since it has religious roots and is still practised today in some parts of India.

Although I am pleased that I was not there then to witness these evil practices, I do regret that I grew up in India without knowing any of these. I had to come to Britain to be enlightened by people like Jean about my own history. Since then, I have continued to research rigorously and learned a lot more, not only about Periyar E.V. Ramasay but also about another social and spiritual activist, Saint Ramalinga Swamigal, known as Vallalar. Vallalar was born in 1823 and the exact date of his death is not known, since he disappeared, just as he had predicted! He lived just two miles from my own native village Kolakkudi, (which is why I write in Tamil under the pen name Kolakkudiyar). Both of these men were active as advocates of social transformation and were very much supported by the British Raj. The discovery that really fascinated me, while researching these two men was their tenacity in attacking the psychological knowledge that is intrinsically interwoven beneath the teachings of Indian religions, justifying the caste division and social discrimination. Vallalar had a very mild approach in tackling this unjust and discriminatory ideology. He advocated a god concept that does not justify any sort of discrimination and he promoted a caste-free society with equality and justice for all. He taught his followers to respect and care for all, including plants and animals. Periyar, who appeared on the scene after Vallalar's time, attacked fearlessly the god concept that justified caste and social discrimination. He started naming and shaming the castes and religious sects, publicly calling them to correct their unjust and discriminatory ideology. His teaching had a huge impact on the whole of India even though he was mainly lecturing in the Tamil language. He was able to do that so boldly because of the support from the British Raj.

I love my Tamil language and take pride in identifying myself as a Tamil Indian. The world became aware of the uniqueness of this classical language, with all its richness, only during the British Raj. The great men who are personally and passionately connected to me are the Italian Jesuit priest Joseph Beschi (1680- 1742), the Irish Congregational missionary Robert Caldwell (1814-1891) and the Canadian Lutheran missionary G.U. Pope (1820-1908) whose father was from Padstow, Cornwall. These people went to my homeland Tamil Nadu in India for missionary service. They started to learn Tamil for their missionary work, but ended up exploring and sharing the rich treasures of the Tamil language and its classically opulent literature to the world. Their discovery, research and contribution have been acknowledged by UNESCO. Their life and work have given a sense of pride and identity to the 77 million Tamils, one of the oldest and largest ethno-linguistic cultural groups in the modern world. These eminent men embraced their life, determined to give their best to the people, language and culture in which they found themselves.

I think colonisation is the wrong word to use for the British presence in India. Evaluating the history and its impact today shows that there was lot more happening between these two countries and people than just commercial interaction. A relationship that had begun through trade, then eventually resulting in the fight for power, transitioned and blossomed into many new forms. The English language, the social, commercial and educational knowledge, British bureaucracy and democratic principles, are the huge legacy that now cement and hold in unity the hard mortar of Indian states with all their difficulties and differences.

In history lessons we were taught how bad the British Raj was towards Indians, but nothing about how barbarously we treated each other, taking shelter and justification in our local religious teachings. I am so fortunate that Jean was there for me to help me see the good side of this complex history. Sadly, there are millions of Indians who are unaware of the positive side of colonisation and continue to harbour feelings of hostility and anger, mostly fuelled by selfish politicians and religious leaders.

Jean was fond of me and very grateful for my ministry. She gave me lovely cards and gifts every Christmas, with many personal touches as shown below in the last card she gave me before she died on 22nd August 2018.

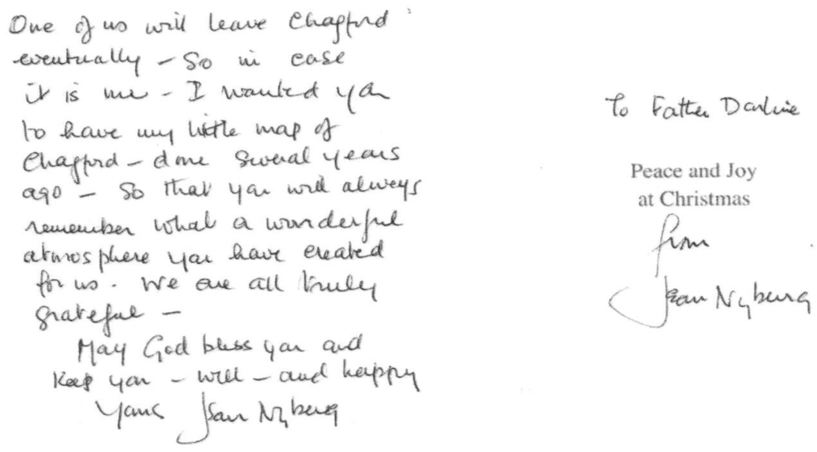

One of us will leave Chagford eventually – So in case it is me – I wanted you to have my little map of Chagford – done several years ago – So that you will always remember what a wonderful atmosphere you have created for us. We are all truly grateful –

May God bless you and keep you – well – and happy

Yours Jean Nyburg

To Father Darlüe

Peace and Joy at Christmas

from

Jean Nyburg

Christmas card written to me by Jean Nyburg in December 2016

As one of the long-standing and pious Catholics of Holy Family, Chagford, Jean had a huge influence on my life as a priest. Although she was increasingly physically frail at the age of 93, for most of the time she was in full command of her mind and her interesting conversation was clear and focussed.

Jean had a good sense of humour, with a gentle smile and caring realism. One Sunday in the autumn of 2015, as I was rushing out of the Church to go to Okehampton for the 11 am Mass, she hurried up to me and said she wanted to confess something important. She said it was about me and she asked me to be brave, so I began to panic a bit yet encouraged her to be quick. She came close and murmured:

"I am sure you are preaching good homilies during Mass, but I couldn't hear a word at the back since my hearing has become so bad". I asked how long that had been going on. She answered, "Since you came to the Parish back in 2011".

I felt very bad and asked her why she hadn't said anything about it before.

She said, "I know everyone here is so happy to have you in the parish and I don't want my personal difficulties to upset you, or anybody else for that matter".

It was that conversation which prompted us to install a PA system with a hearing loop facility. Sadly, just a few months later Jean was confined to her flat due to her restricted mobility. Reflecting on the whole event, I thought how virtuous she was. To be totally selfless is something I find hard, but it came to Jean quite naturally. Mahatma Gandhi might well have met women like Jean, which is why he made this powerful statement: "Man can never be a woman's equal in the spirit of selfless service with which nature has endowed her".

I was a direct beneficiary of Jean's admirable selflessness, coupled with her genuine care and generosity. She arranged for me to go to the Indian Restaurant in Chagford when it first opened. Initially she and I were to go there for lunch, but a few days later she phoned to say that she would pay for dinner for two, but she excused herself saying she would be an inadequate match for me. She insisted I find another parishioner or a friend, if possible similar to my age, to join me for an evening meal. The following day she gave me the money for the dinner but the hunt for the appropriate dinner partner was still ongoing. I went through the list of parishioners with her expecting her to suggest a match. As she had been there longer than any other parishioner, she knew most of them well with some details of their history too. We had a little healthy gossip about our parishioners and she had something nice to say about each person while wittingly throwing some critical comments in a very gentle manner.

When I suggested someone from the list, she said, 'Yes you could go with this person but just be prepared as you may be bored by the aimless chatter. You really want to enjoy the evening, don't you?'

At last she accepted my suggestion that I should go for the meal with a particular person, which I did the following week. Reflecting back, it occurred to me how she naturally and spontaneously began to care, not only for my physical needs with food and drink, but also for my psychological wellbeing by ensuring the right person with whom to socialise.

As a Doctoral researcher and a student of Professor Paul Howard-Jones, the world-renowned brain and behaviour study specialist, I began to look into Jean's good character more scientifically. I wanted to explore if there is any link between Jean's strong 'Cradle Catholic' faith and the virtuous behaviour that came to her so effortlessly. I came in contact with a number of fascinating neuroscience research papers, a summary of which is shared below.

Evolving brains are said to produce minds. Minds operate on creative, insightful and imaginary entities, so they can produce not only those that are physical but also emotional. Physical human beings are not only rational but also emotional. Religion and spirituality are part of an evolving culture of human emotions and imagination. Although it is difficult to empirically discover and prove the physical existence of a deity, the emotional impact on human life is so strong that it has become part of an evolving brain. These are scientifically observable and can be measured. For example, belief in spirits, fairies and angels producing positive and healthy value is important for social wellbeing and it does strengthen the evolutionary fitness (Henneberg & Saniotis, 2009). Emotions are strongly influenced by neurohormonal regulations and trigger imagination which forms the bulk of religious experiences. Over the period of evolution this process could have contributed to memory improvement and the ability to process more information in the central nervous system accompanied by emotional experience. It might seem to be 'illogical' or 'irrational' brain activity, but it has a positive adaptive value by providing motivation to behave in a socially acceptable manner (Previc, 2006). For example, one could dedicate one's whole life to be at the service of a community, with the conviction that you have been called by God to do a job, which could in religion be termed as a 'mission' or 'a call of duty'. It is also argued that over the period of brain evolution, mental image and emotional experience became part of human culture and survival, since they contributed to wellness, irrespective of whether they were reflective of reality or not (Henneberg & Saniotis, 2009). It is noticeable in history, that some of the major components of life such as art, music, architecture, education and morality started to evolve around religion and in turn religion evolved around them. Emergence of management, leadership, structures and institutions within religion gave concrete expression to the mutual evolution impacting both religious and psychological life (Kuhn, 1962). This evolutionary origin of human brain and religious spirituality explains how Jean's Catholic faith could have contributed to her virtuous life.

People like Jean and her virtuous way of life are rapidly decreasing in the world due to religions and their teachings being neglected, ignored and in some cases even ridiculed by attractive, opposing arguments. It is a historical fact that there have been wars, crimes, scandals and abuses in the name of religions, but the goodness they have brought outweighs all the bad. In my view, the end of religions would be the end of virtuous life in humans, which would eventually lead to our permanent extinction from the planet earth.

Christianity, especially the Catholic Church, is moving faster than other religions in the world, teaching and at the same time learning lessons both from the past and the present.

Reference

Henneberg, M., & Saniotis, A. (2009). Evolutionary origins of human brain and spirituality. *Anthropologischer Anzeiger, 67*(4), 427-438. Retrieved from <Go to ISI>://WOS:000276579800008. doi:10.1127/0003-5548/2009/0032

Kuhn, T. S. (1962): The structure of scientific revolutions. University of Chicago.

Previc, F. H. (2006). *The role of the extrapersonal brain systems in religious activity.*
Consciousness and Cognition, 15(3), 500-539.

6. Revd Michael Reynolds' burning bush

It was around 6 am on Thursday 22nd June 2017 the phone rang. Whenever the phone rings at that sort of time I expect something unexpected, and it proved to be so. Mrs Janet Reynolds, Michael's wife apologised for ringing so early in the morning but continued to say that there was a serious fire accident at Michael's house. My immediate question was about his safety. She replied, 'I knew you would ask me that' and confirmed that Michael and his dog had been winched out of the first floor of the house with the help of neighbours and the firefighters.

As soon as I finished talking to Janet, I rang Michael and spoke to him for few minutes expressing how sorry I was. He sounded very shaken, and I could sense he needed someone to be with him other than the ambulance crew and the firefighters. After Mass at Holy Family Church in Chagford, I cancelled my trip to the university and drove straight to his house in Beaworthy. The memory of the Grenfell Tower fire tragedy just a week beforehand was still fresh in my mind. The country had just mourned the death of 72 people and many others were injured both physically and psychologically. While I was driving to Michael's house, I prayed silently that the trauma that he may have experienced should not cause him any harm. Nearing his house, I smelt the smoke although the fire fighters had completely doused the fire and made the house safe to enter to collect any items that could be saved.

For a while Michael was visibly down, but he regained his priestly spirit and appreciation of how blessed he felt to have been alive rather than seeing the accident as a curse with a high possibility of death. I responded by echoing his feelings in the following words,

"It sounds like you had a 'burning bush experience' (Exodus 3:1-4:17) like Moses on Mount Horeb where the bush was on fire but was not consumed by the flames."

Michael was able to smile and responded, 'Indeed, my dog and I were spared from being consumed by the flames'.

There was no place to sit since the whole area was dotted with debris, so we walked around talking. I had never been in a situation such as this and so was struggling to find words to empathise with him. However, I sensed that Michael was appreciative of my presence and understood how much I felt for him at this traumatic time. In fact, I felt strengthened by his ability to cope with the tragic accident and so I gently asked if he needed anything to be done for him immediately. Without any hesitation Michael, a successful priest himself, asked for prayers. I said a spontaneous prayer standing in the midst of the burnt down house, asking the Lord for his strength and blessing. The prayer lasted only couple of minutes, and immediately after the prayer Michael seemed to be more confident. I too felt the power of prayer and began to feel less anxious than before.

Prayer has been the heartbeat of my priesthood. Michael has expressed the same about his priesthood too on several occasions. I consider the Divine Mercy prayer group in our Parish the lifeline and the most important of all groups, since it forms the basis of everything we do in the Parish. Michael has been a huge supporter of this group.

As a psychologist I have studied neuroscience theoretically and have experienced it through prayers in action practically. Aloud prayer, using words rather than visualisation techniques, is mostly used in meditation as it activates the prefrontal cortex of the brain - the region responsible for willful behaviour, executive functions and decision-making. I was also aware of the implicit non-verbal communication between right brain to right brain, which means that silent prayers in the presence of others can evoke powerful emotions in the person prayed for. I have a strong feeling that Michael was able to feel the power of my silent prayers too.

Whether said loudly or silently, prayer is one of the scientifically proven health treatments for body and spirit that doesn't have any bad side effects. All it takes is little bit of effort and lots of goodwill. "The Lord is near to all who call on him, to all who call on him in truth and prayer" (Psalm 145:18).

Michael's son Kit had arrived just before me and was trying to clear some of the items saved from the fire.

Michael's house immediately after the fire accident on Thursday 22nd June 2017

I was in my spotless white clerical collar shirt worn for Mass at Chagford that morning but offered to join in to help with the clearing.

The clearing that Father Darline helped to move

The clear up took over an hour and I noticed that, as my white shirt was getting dirty, my conscience was emerging clean. I wanted to show my faith in tangible action but didn't know how to other than show my empathy and try to console Michael. I knew from the time I was ordained, that I should be a priest not for myself but for others. This realisation was the driving force behind my pastoral adventures, making myself available as much as possible all to all, following the example of Saint Paul.

I asked Michael if I could thank the neighbours involved with his rescue and he took me to them. They were kind people and welcomed us with a cup of tea and biscuits. I stayed there until it was time for lunch while Michael was describing the entire ordeal. From my counselling psychology I knew the power of listening and its healing benefits and I was beginning to feel that power. I was able to offer my listening ear, and at the same time I felt the relief he was experiencing by talking about his traumatic accident.

I always recommend that couples train themselves to listen as listening is key to a successful relationship and a happy life. Listening increases understanding, so it is the most important component for problem solving. 'A person of understanding delights in wisdom' (Proverb 10:23).

Listening is harder than speaking, which is why people generally jump into conversations. Sometimes we see people cutting across a conversation before the other person has finished. That's because impatience is associated with chitchat, while patience is associated with listening. Good listening is real and personal; it involves listening to conscience, intuition, body and soul.

Listening is a skill that some people have as a natural gift, while others have to work to acquire it. When I became a priest, I thought I had the natural ability to listen, but later discovered I was more of a speaker than a listener and so had to work hard to be a listener - especially when I first started to train as a psychologist. I remember how difficult it was to learn to listen. Now I find it is the most useful tool in my personal and professional life.

Listening helps to know oneself and the other better, especially in the face of confusion and uncertainty. Listening is therapeutic and is one of the most powerful aids to healing. That is the reason that I prioritise visiting my parishioners in hospital. I say very little after my prayers and most of the time I just sit by their side and listen. Listening offers hope and respect to the person who speaks and empowers them with confidence and comfort.

It aids healing in all aspects of life.

I spent over two hours at Michael's place and as he was walking me to my car he said, "Thanks be to God for the gift of faith that has made your presence possible here with me at this time of need".

This statement struck me powerfully and I reflected on it as I was driving home. The faith offered by Christianity is so powerful. It has shaped my life and I have seen the lives of many others shaped by it.

I am aware there is so much confusion out in the world, with conflicting ideas and views about relationships and values. Sometimes there is a struggle as to which one to follow. Having studied religious pluralism and the history of world religions, I believe there is no other religion like Christianity that offers its followers "the burning bush experience" – an experience that means being an integral part of the burning world yet maintaining an unique identity of being a true Christian without being completely consumed by it.

7. My Friend Dave's Enviable Faith

Meeting on 2nd March 2014

Meeting with David was one of the most challenging, reflective and learning experiences that I have ever had as a Priest.

From my first meeting it was obvious that Dave knew very well that his death was just round the corner.

I am used to handling the grief stricken, the depressed and the lonely. However, I must admit I used to feel bit nervous when it came to handling intense emotions. Later I discovered it has been so due to the impact of my own Tamil classic Culture which had shaped its people for over 5000 years with a rich literature surging with emotions.

Dave's situation was totally different. He was neither grief stricken nor depressed. He looked well, sounded clear and listened intently. It was my first experience dealing with a person awaiting imminent death. Although I knew his condition, when I heard him expressing it to me it spurred tumults of various emotions in me.

Quiet sorrow filled my eyes with tears. Helpless rage stilled my heart with fears. Questions of why and how such a nice person should be taken away from the world so soon deflated my desire for saving souls. Stinging feelings of distress and pain took over my instincts of priestly loyalty and pastoral bravery.

Having been inundated with these emotions, I felt as if I was going through a dark tunnel, eventually drowning beneath the shallow waters. Feeling shaken to the core of my being, I spurred myself on, regulating my emotions, to offer Dave the required pastoral care and support. I began taking deep breaths, asking Dave what he was feeling at that moment in time. He started thanking me for sparing time to be with him and then proceeded to say how grateful he was to God for all the love, care and good time that he had with Monica his wife, the children, grand-children and his life in general, in spite of his cancer.

I decided not to have any thematic direction for our conversation and to move along with whatever emerged. But, surprisingly, Dave was directional, specific and articulate. I thought this came to him without much effort. Later I realised he was a musician by profession and would have used these skills for better coordination and successful performance.

He confessed openly that he was not a regular church goer but never missed an opportunity to get to church if he had one. Dave said he was never an obstacle to Monica's Catholicism and continued by saying how he was envious of her faith at times. I was reminded of what Aristotle said about envy, 'Envy is a pain at the sight of such a good fortune'. Dave's envy was not a pain but a feeling of missed cheer. He did regard Monica's faith a real fortune with which she had pulled through successfully not only her battle with Cancer but also other challenging times in her life. He was convinced nothing could have been more a powerful tool than her faith which had empowered her to be gently resolute against all odds.

Within the first few minutes of my conversation with him I realised how deeply he valued the faith and believed in its impact. Having listened to my homilies during a couple of funerals at St. Boniface, he amiably requested me to explain about death and resurrection. I paused for a while reminding myself not to respond in a high - handed theologian's unyielding dogmatic style expecting incontestable surrender. He knew me well as someone who usually simplifies faith and its practice. He confirmed this at the start of his question.

I started explaining death as the normal end of life and that we believe when one dies with Christ's grace, it is a participation in the death and resurrection of the Lord. He was very quick to ask how one can die with Christ's grace. The explanation that I gave was very simple; 'Dave you are qualified for that, because if one is not able to live in Christ, it is very difficult to die in Christ. Therefore, from your sharing about your support to Monica and the children and the grandchildren, it is very clear you have made every attempt to live in Christ, although you did not have the official banner on you as a regular Church going Christian. He immediately came in with the sub-question of why should one practise faith by going to church regularly and actively participate in church related events. He continued, most of the people like me try to be a good husband or father or grandfather or friend or neighbour. Are you suggesting that that is enough to call oneself living in Christ?

I had to be careful not to amplify my doctrinal knowledge about faith and its various expressions but rather use ordinary language to explain faith and the transcendence of God.

My reply included explanations about why we have pious practices. Apart from the theological significance, they are given as tools through which our efforts to become good people are enriched.

Jesus came preaching, intending to make us all good. He asked people to love, repent, forgive, be honest, sincere and faithful. To realise these virtues, after Jesus, we have established structures in the form of religion, and churches with rules to enhance that process. Christianity does not teach these virtues from imagination but from the inspirational revelation received through our tradition and the sacred scripture (the Bible). For example, the Mass we celebrate every day is born from tradition and sacred scripture.

Dave came in at this point 'Oh yes, it answers my question about why there should be some level of preparation before one could become a Christian or a Catholic'. Acknowledging his answer, I proceeded further giving an example of how Monica, his wife, has been actively involving in preparation of our Parish children for Holy Communion and Confirmation. During the period of preparation, the importance and significance of faith and its bearing on our life are discussed as an indispensable part of our existence.

Dave acknowledged this explanation with a smile and a nod in agreement, yet enquired why still some people don't like established structures of religion. I knew what was at the back of his mind when he asked this question. It was really a sad and challenging time for not only the Catholic Church but also for the whole of Christianity, facing allegations of historical abuses and scandals all over the developed world.

I took no time to respond since I was aware of the problem both as an outsider as well as an insider. I said, 'The church is divine but managed by humans. Even God is let down by humans sometimes'. It is really sad.

As humans we tend to blame God for our own faults. Dave said quietly 'I have made some mistakes in life but I shall not blame God or anybody for them'. I was very much moved by his simple and yet honest act of contrition.

He expressed his wish to die in peace without causing any more discomfort to anybody, especially Monica his wife. In all our meetings his boundless love for Monica was explicitly made clear with a rare mix of worry and joy.

He was worried because life without him would seem unusual and different for Monica. He said, through his own life experience, he knew how some partners got irrevocably lost at the death of the other partner. His wish was that this would never happen to Monica. He was happy for her because he said, 'her Catholic faith would save her' from any possible disaster.

We ended our meeting with the agreement to meet up later.

I came back to the presbytery thinking how extraordinary Dave was. The firm, solid and rock like faith was not something new in him. He might have probably been living it throughout his life in an unassuming way while Monica had opportunities to express it outwardly through her engagement with the Catholic Church. I was just fortunate to learn his hidden treasure, the strong yet silent faith that motivated him to be a loving husband, responsible dad and caring grandpa. That evening I prayed to God to grant me the simple, unassuming yet the enviable faith of Dave.

Meeting on 14th April, 11th and 17th May 2014

The major themes that dominated the rest of our meetings except the last one was the controversial theme of "No Salvation Outside the Church" and the idea of 'Happy Death'.

Dave requested me to explain how I could assert that his possible death is in Christ while we have the commonly held belief in 'No Salvation Outside the Church'. I remember this was very well explained to us at the Pontifical Institute by the most liked priest Father K J Thomas (who was murdered on 31st March 2013 and the accused included, sadly, four Catholic priests and a number of laity in Bangaluru Archdiocese, India). Fr. K J Thomas was a competent tutor who used to simplify complications and this approach had a tremendous influence on me then as well as later in my ministry and academia.

This slogan 'No Salvation outside the Church' had a huge success in motivating the missionaries and the people with primitive religious backgrounds for evangelisation purposes. Inevitably It had also faced failure since it was understood to imply belittling the non-Catholics.

I started in my usual way with Dave looking back into the history of this slogan specifically starting with the Faith of the early Fathers. It was a peak moment of heresies running rampant and therefore this assertion had to be forceful for the intended audience. It was never intended to exclude, but to include as many people as possible since this doctrine has been based on the belief that "all salvation comes from Christ the Head".

I tried to simplify it in one sentence: Anyone with God-Good-Conscience would be saved.

'This affirmation is not aimed at those who, through no fault of their own, do not know Christ and his Church: Those who, through no fault of their own, do not know the Gospel of Christ or his Church, but who nevertheless seek God with a sincere heart, and, moved by grace, try in their actions to do his will as they know it through the dictates of their conscience—those too may achieve eternal salvation' (CCC 847).

Dave was very much pleased with my explanation and expressed his appreciation and sympathy to Catholicism for succeeding as the fastest growing religion in the world in spite of unnecessary scornful scrutiny at times.

This brought us to the final topic of our meetings; the 'Happy Death'.

As we began our conversation on the topic, I did warn him jokingly that pastoral care such as mine usually delays the desired demise. Instantly he replied with urgency, "No, I don't want to prolong mine anymore causing concerns to all around me especially my wife Monica". However, he did outlive the D tors predicted time limit.

One specific request that he made every so often during all our meetings was to pray for his peaceful and speedy death.

Whenever he mentioned the word 'death', I observed in him an intricate fusion of intense sorrow with serenity and tranquillity. I had never come across such a situation of deep conflicting emotions in some one faced with inevitable death. He was upholding all the virtues of Man.

I felt completely astonished and to some extent powerless, not because

I was suffering from thanatophobia (fear of death) or necrophobia (fear of dying person) but of his disposition of heart and mind. I thought there was a lot for me to take in for rest of my life from Dave; to be considerate, optimistic, selfless and above all to be a really good human being.

****

I was indeed fortunate to be by the side of Dave praying for the repose of his soul a few minutes after his death on 17th May 2014.

Dave's sober bravery in facing the reality of faith and death had taught me something more than I had been learning all these years in academia.

****

8. Win Male: Good Atheists and Inhuman Spiritualists

It was the feast of Epiphany, Sunday 5th January 2014, and, after all my Masses in the morning, I did some office work and was happy to have cleared all my papers from the desk in the afternoon.

I wanted to go to bed early as the following day, Monday, I had planned a lot of work for my PhD thesis. I took myself to bed around 9.45 pm and was feeling the comfortable warmth of the duvet as I was fading away in to sleep.

The phone rang five minutes after I got into the bed and I was bit late reaching the phone so the answer machine kicked in to take the message. I then heard the desperate, sobbing voice of Monica Ovens from Sticklepath saying "Win Male has had a fire accident in her house".

I jumped out of bed to reach the phone before she completed the message, apologising to Monica for being late in reaching the phone and promised to be on the spot in a few minutes time. I know the roads very well having used them as an alternative to the A30 to Chagford every week for Mass, especially whenever I felt like being cheered up after all my psychology research.

I was accompanied by Monica Ovens every time I visited Win. Monica used to wait for me just before the Sticklepath village shop. As soon as I arrived she would get into my car and accompany me to Win's house, which was only a few hundred yards away.

On that fateful day, I had to drive without Monica and as I was driving into Willey Lane leading to Win's house, I could see a number of Police cars parked at the side of the road.

I drove slowly, passing the Police and the emergency vehicles, until I was blocked by a huge Fire truck. I could not park my car on the side of the road as there were too many Police cars so I just left my car in the middle of the road and got out so as to be seen by some one.

Monica spotted me immediately and came to me with eyes full of tears.

She said, "Thank you Father for coming out at this time of the night" and she broke down. I could hear her grief and desperation as she continued in a frail voice, "There was a fire in Win's house."

I asked immediately "Is Win saf. and alive?"

Monica said something which I could not hear as we were surrounded by a lot of Firefighters and Police. As we were walking towards the house where Win lived, the Chief Police officer and the Chief Fire Officer were kind and polite to both of us and respected our wish to pray for Win. They asked us to wait for a while until they had completed their procedures.

I started to shiver and shake as I did not have enough woollies on. I had not stopped to put on my usual thermal wear as I thought that I would be late reaching the house.

The Chief Fire Officer came back to us within few minutes and expressed his regret that it would not be possible for me to see Win as she had been badly burned and as a result she had died.

Monica broke down again and was upset at the Officer's refusal. I stepped in with the hope of convincing the Officer saying Win had been a pious Catholic with intense love for her Faith. I continued my request to the Officer to allow me nearer the house so that I could pray for her and hopefully bring reasonable peace after the miserable death that she had to endure.

The Officer agreed to that suggestion and asked me to follow him, while Monica had to wait nearer the fire trucks. As I was walking behind the Fire Officer I saw dozens of police and fire service men still clearing the debris from the fire. I was advised to watch my step as there were lots of hoses running along the pavements.

Halfway there a few police officers joined us and followed me to the house. The Fire Officer showed me a place in front of the house and advised me to stand there to do the prayers for Win. I stood dumbfounded for few minutes filled with the shock of her sudden death.

Grief and sadness filled me as I kept looking at the burned down roof. I was taken there to pray but I could not. Instead my mind was filled with past memories. In this very same place I had visited Win on the 23rd December 2013, along with Monica and we had a lovely chat with the usual laughter for nearly an hour.

After a while I turned back slowly and to my surprise, I noticed there were a dozen Police and Fire men standing motionless watching me and I turned back to my previous position and continued the spontaneous prayer:

"Lord, we thank you for the gift of life to Win, with which she enlightened so many people. Now bless her and grant her the place that she really deserves in your kingdom. Amen".

After that simple prayer, I threw the Holy Water as far as I could into her house through the holes burned by the fire as I was aware that the body of Win was still inside her house.

I slowly moved back from the main door to where the Police and Fire personnel were waiting for me. They followed me to my car where Monica was anxiously waiting to know whether I had seen Win's body. Although she was disappointed with my negative answer, she gained some relief when I told her that I was able to pray and bless Win while standing in front of the house.

Monica was full of gratitude for me having come out at that time of the night.

I said to her "That is what we priests are for".

It was almost 11 pm as I was driving back to the Presbytery and a lot of unique memories of Win crossed my mind, especially her honest and straight forward opinions about the infallibility of the Pope in the Catholic Church and women priesthood in the Anglican Church.

Two days later Peter Male, Win's son, rang me and introduced himself as an Atheist. After I expressed my condolences to him, we agreed to meet up here in the Presbytery at Okehampton on 8th January after the usual 10 am Mass.

I was dreading our meeting a bit, as Peter had said he was an Atheist and I thought the meeting with him would be a difficult challenge. As a Psychologist, I had lot of ideas to make Peter feel at home with me during the meeting the next day but my confusion was how to proceed or where to begin.

As I went to bed my mind was full of good thoughts and I was picking and choosing from these to use the next day during our proposed meeting.

On the 8th January the 10 am Mass was offered for Win Male.

After the Service I was surprised, as I saw Peter, accompanied by his son's partner, Jennie, on the CCTV camera. I thought it could be the beginning of a miracle. They were going to the Church door even though the Presbytery door was nearer to where they had parked their car in the drive.

Peter, having introduced himself as an Atheist, had the opportunity to see Our Lady's statue at the entrance and the Crucified Jesus in the middle of the Church before seeing me.   Usually, people, familiar or unfamiliar, who have appointments with me go to the Presbytery first but in Peter's case it was different. He went straightaway to the Church.

I thought within myself that it was indeed a miracle that he went into the Church before we had the meeting. Just a few seconds later, I hurried down to the Church to meet him.

Unlike other meetings, the meeting with Peter and Jennie took an hour and forty-five minutes. It was indeed a fantastic experience of sharing good thoughts about Win and how religion becomes important to people in their lives. We hardly had any heated discussion or difference of opinion. It was the most peaceful funeral preparatory meeting that I have ever had in the Parish. The most striking moment of our meeting was Peter shedding tears over the prayers that I said when I was at Win's house on that fateful night. I had to repeat the prayer to them from my memory at the request of Jennie, his partner.

Peter agreed to almost all my suggestions to have a full blown Roman Catholic funeral service for his mother. I started to reflect how sometimes atheists are perceived and interpreted by believers as people who are totally against everything that the religion stands for.

I came to realise that there are very good, humane and flexible Atheists as well as inhuman, rigid Spiritualists in the world.

What a strange world we live in!

9. Peter Benson Bayfield's simple and yet powerful faith

It was on Thursday 4th April 2013 around 1 am when the phone rang. It was Maureen Bayfield and she apologised for phoning in the middle of the night. Although it was only my second year in the Parish, I knew Peter and Maureen quite well as a devout Catholic couple and so was aware Maureen would not ring me at night unless it was something urgent. I acknowledged her apology and encouraged her to speak. In a choking voice she told me the sad news of the death of her husband Peter. After offering my condolences, I promised to be with her within 30 minutes.

I drove the 6.5 miles to Exbourne, the village where Peter and Maureen lived. Although I had driven around many Devon villages, it was a difficult and dark drive that night with no lights from Okehampton town until I reached Exbourne village.

The satnav guided me to the village but wasn't accurate enough to identify their house, High Tumbles. I drove up and down the village but couldn't see any sign of their house. I initially hesitated to call for directions as I thought it would be inappropriate to disturb someone whose husband had just passed away, but when I did try to call, I was disappointed to see there was no network signal on my mobile phone. I drove to the side of St Mary's Church and said a decade of rosary. Halfway through my prayers I was inspired to drive out of the village with the hope of getting a signal.

Although in shock Maureen managed to direct me and turned on the inside and outside lights so that I would be able to find the house without too much difficulty. I silenced my satnav to follow Maureen's instructions and prayed resolutely that I should be able to find my way. As I prayed, I spotted her house right in front of me.

I was taken straight to Peter's room. He had just passed away and looked as peaceful and serene as he did at Church on Sundays. I prayed over him and we spent some time sitting around Peter's bed as Maureen recalled the good times they had had in life and how grateful she was for them. She was able to spontaneously steer her feelings in a manageable way although I found it difficult to contain my feelings for the loss and grief she was suffering. I struggled to find the correct vocabulary to communicate how much I felt for her but spent the next four hours with her until her son John arrived early in the morning.

Although I had difficulty finding the words to empathise, Maureen knew I was there for her. Her way of coping with such significant loss was to be grateful for all the blessings she had received so far in life, which I found quite extraordinary and edifying.

The Marie Curie nurse was also present with us. She was a wonderful person and I could sense her deep empathy for Maureen. Although she wasn't particularly religious and didn't respond to the prayers, she had a powerful presence with positive vibes. Her presence was a helpful supplement to Maureen's process of loss and grief. She did not identify herself as a Christian, but she was truly a Christian in every way she conducted herself that night.

I have seen people like that nurse in my clinical as well as academic circles. They are genuinely very good people, who like some of my loyal and wonderful friends, do not want to identify with Christianity or any other religion. They often say that the reason is mostly historical. I personally feel that no other religion has become such an integral part of human civilisation as Christianity. Every aspect of human existence has been impacted by Christian traditions and teachings - be it family, social life or the realms of education, economics, politics, history and even a few of the other religions in the world.

People who focus on the negative impacts of Christianity advocate its total dismissal, and resort to anti-Christian ideology, finding shelter in atheism or agnosticism. Some of those people base their arguments largely on historical and empirical evidence gathered from the past which include abuse of power and authority, demonisation of other religions, crusades, Inquisition, harmful rigidity and unkind authoritarianism. They mock some of the auditory and visual experiences as pathology and hallucinations when they are claimed as divine apparitions. Unhappy with such a reality, Karl Marx described religion as 'the opium of the people', while Friedrich

Nietzsche said, "The word 'Christianity' is already a misunderstanding - in reality there has been only one Christian, and he died on the Cross".

It is hard to ignore their arguments since these are born out of the worst, most embarrassing and damaging historical episodes of Christianity.

On the other hand, the positive effects of Christianity are plentiful. Christian ethos form the essential basis of western democracy. Its influence on global art, music, philosophy and culture is enormous. Christianity was the major pioneer in the alleviation of hunger, poverty and illiteracy in the world. Its missionaries went to the remotest frontiers of the world and spent all their lives amongst the needy; in most cases they died there, with far more emphasis on social services than spreading the Gospel, even though the latter was their main mandate. Christianity's insightful role in the eradication of cannibalism and its rigorous emphasis on the importance of monogamy were significant milestones in moving humanity into a more civilised society. Christianity has been the safe guardian and promoter of social and moral order. In the recent past no other religion has been as quick as Christianity to put its house in order when challenged on issues that concern humanity.

When comparing both the positive and the negative impacts created by Christianity, I think the positive outweighs the negative. Atheism and its ideology have an attractive theory but it fails to address humans' practical concerns. Recent neurological studies explain how human brains have evolved with an innate longing for supernatural power. Failure to address that longing, results in psychological illness and breakdown in social and moral order (McCullough, 1995).

What we find today in the western world, and especially in the UK, is a rapid decline in church-goers and Christian ethos, with a rise in knife crime, teenage pregnancy, relationship breakdown, children forced into foster care and young people getting lost in drug and alcohol addiction as well as radicalisation through destructive ideologies. The efforts to address these challenges by social and community services are at breaking point. It seems important, and even necessary, to dig into the much-ignored treasure trove of Christian values and ethos which has the potential to make our affluent nation joyous and successful. I think there is so much truth in what

G. K. Chesterton said: "The Christian ideal has not been tried and found wanting. It has been found difficult; and left untried."

Christianity is moving faster than other religions in the world, in line with the worlds of science and technology, teaching and learning lessons both from the past and the present to promote a virtuous life. The best example is Pope Francis who recently said, "Since many of you do not belong to the Catholic Church and others are non-believers, from the bottom of my heart I give this silent blessing to each and every one of you, respecting the conscience of each one of you but knowing that each one of you is a child of God".

Christianity is the world's biggest religion with 2.1 billion followers. It has an ancient and admirable history intertwined with human civilisation and its survival. It is still the fastest growing religion in the world in spite of heavy-handed suppression by those who do not like Christianity.

Although there are a few who dispute the theological explanation for such an enduring survival, everyone tends to agree on the historical fact that Christianity's successful survival has been due to its pioneering efforts dealing with poverty, conflict and disaster caused by humans and nature. Principles of charity and temperance were prevailing virtues of the early Christians in the first century. They were taught to give expression to their faith through 'good deeds' (Charity).

It is estimated that there are just over 400,000 Christian charities in the world including CAFOD, Christian Aid, Christian Vision, Christians Against Poverty and All churches Trust. Locally the Okehampton United Charities engage with those who need support, working in charitable service beyond the confines of religion and race. It is a matter of pride for us to celebrate the fact that there are now many so-called 'non-Christian' organisations and charities sharing the 'good deeds' that 'Christians' began.

We do come across individuals and groups happily identifying themselves as atheists, non-believers, non-Church goers and Seasonal/Occasional/Vocational Church goers, yet actively engaging in 'good deeds' as well as the cardinal virtues of prudence, justice, fortitude, and temperance. Whatever may be the ideological and personal explanation they give to their distinct identity, we who call ourselves Christians are invited to remember Jesus' saying, 'Do not stop him; for whoever is not against you is for you' (Luke 9:50).

The Marie Curie nurse who attended on Peter was certainly not against us; she communicated her empathy in every way. However, I think there is a huge benefit in frequenting church and the practice of faith as vividly seen in the lives of Peter and Maureen. They were pious Catholics, devoted to the church and each other and well-liked by people in the parish. Maureen was awarded the Saint Boniface Diocesan Medal for her outstanding work in the parish, and I found working with her both pleasant and rewarding. They were married for over 50 years and had four children; Julie Ann, Tina, Teresa and John. I thought they were a special couple in some ways, because they both had the same style of conducting themselves - moderate in speech, serene in appearance, and thoughtful in conversation. This is a common pattern with successful and happy couples that I have observed all over the world. A true practice of faith offers opportunities for regular learning and growth. It increases self-awareness, which is at the heart of interpersonal relationships.

Self-awareness is the conscious knowledge of oneself: personality, emotions, beliefs, strengths and weaknesses. A lack of self-awareness is one of the main causes of conflict and failure in relationships and in life, leading to an increase in crime and mental health issues. People lacking self-awareness sadly suffer, trapping themselves in misery and blaming their failures on fate.

The notion of self-awareness has been around for a long time. It captured the attention of the ancient Greek philosopher, Socrates, who said "My friend... care for your psyche...know thyself, for once we know ourselves, we may learn how to care for ourselves". As members of a civilised society, we are duty bound to care for each other and self-awareness is based on that conviction.

Unbiased, objective self-awareness helps us recognise and understand our strengths and limitations as well as those of others. People with high levels of self-awareness usually have successful relationships and are often good leaders and great achievers. Almost every self-help book, professional development course or guide to happy and successful living places heavy emphasis on the need for self-awareness.

Long before any of these modern approaches, the Bible gave valuable insights into this vital concept. The Psalmist, in the process of self-awareness, cried "Why are you downcast, O my soul? Why so disturbed within me?" (Psalm 42:5,11, 43:5). Advising the Romans, St. Paul wrote "Do not think of yourself more highly than you ought, but rather think of yourself with sober judgement" (Rom 12:3).

Meditation and acts of contrition are tools that lead towards self-awareness. Christianity, particularly the Catholic church, offers plenty of opportunities for that. All that it needs is to take oneself to a Church and look out for them.

Maureen and Peter were devout Catholics and gave their best to the Parish and at the same time questioned gently in a caring way about the changes I introduced. Sometimes there is a misunderstanding about being a good Christian. It is not endorsing strict adherence and conformity all the time. It is all about the love and care and the intentions behind the questions that are asked. Maureen and Peter had the best of intentions for the Catholic church and for me personally in the Parish.

Questioning the religious/Christian/Catholic faith used to be considered anathema and the undeclared norm, 'Pay, Pray and Obey' was expected with strict adherence, and praised when conformity was endorsed. In contrast we find in the scriptures Jesus asked 135 questions, most of which are against the established structures of his time such as 'You brood of vipers, how can you who are evil say anything good?' (Matthew 12:34).

I remember once we had a 'Question and Answer' session on Faith in the Parish Hall which lasted for two hours. I felt anxious at the beginning but eventually got used to it. Those of us who gathered for the session on that day were aware of past history. Interestingly they are the people who practice regularly and maintain absolute adherence to doctrine and the demands of faith, yet had the ardent desire to deepen their understanding by caring critique. None of us felt those two hours were heavy in any way and in fact experienced the opposite. Many expressed a desire for more sessions in the future.

Our session discussing faith did go very deep into science, history, tradition, scripture and culture. All these have been instrumental in shaping not only just religious faith but also our humanity. We found adequate reasons to rejoice and at the same time we came to a meaningful and generous understanding of what we can and cannot change. However, we felt the need for newer, better and more acceptable ways to cater for modern minds and hearts.

Correct understanding of religious faith and its constructive practice can promote a life of liberty, respect, tolerance and love. For this reason, questioning the faith is necessary. As Albert Einstein would say, 'Learn from yesterday, live for today, hope for tomorrow. The important thing is not to stop questioning'.

Maureen used to be one of the first ones to arrive at the Church since she had multiple roles in the parish. She was the principal Organist, organised the choir and was also involved with cleaning and doing flowers. Peter would sit at the far end of the Church quietly praying and I would talk with him before most people arrived. He would give a gentle smile and thank me for my presence and ministry in the Parish. He once asked me, "What made you come to this country with its cold, windy, miserable weather?". My response was just one word, 'Priesthood,' and he replied, "That is what the church and this country need now".

People like Peter were instrumental in building my trust and confidence on a pastoral/personal level as well as public/civic level and I began to engage in both comprehensively. When Cllr Paul Vachon, the then (2014) Mayor of Okehampton, asked me to be his Chaplain, I said I needed a couple of days to make my decision. I did extensive research and discovered the level of dedication, care and concern that the town council had for the wellbeing of the town's people and its environment. So, despite the time constraints of my parish ministry and my extensive academic involvement, I decided to take up the opportunity to be part of this welfare-caring community.

I attended some of the town meetings and going through the agendas and minutes, chatting with the Mayor, the councilors and many people, I found that one thing stood out quite remarkably - the desire for common good. My admiration for Britain has grown stronger since I realised how this desire is entrenched in the fabric of British culture and history, and how both nationally and globally, it has made Britain's presence 'great'. I have felt many a time that people living in Britain are extremely blessed and fortunate.

In spite of the expenses scandal, Transparency International's statistics prove our politicians are far cleaner and cleverer than many in the developed and developing world. In spite of the controversial waiting times, the NHS is rated as one of the best health systems in the world. In spite of the unpleasant spending cuts, Britain's social care, education, and emergency services deserve their accolade as the 'best life-saving custodians of the people in the world'.

The BBC, the world's oldest and largest broadcaster, is applauded for impartiality and objectivity in spite of the criticism of being part of the Establishment. In spite of the allegations of abuses and scandals, the Christian leaders and the faithful here strive constantly to profess and practise their faith in a more exemplary and conscientious way than many in the world.

Great Britain, despite its challenges and failures, has a compelling desire to succeed as a nation. We can all draw inspiration from Winston Churchill's quote "Success consists of going from failure to failure without loss of enthusiasm".

Christianity, more especially Catholicism, provides plenty of opportunities for enthusiasm which is what helped Maureen to cope with the loss of Peter and continue to inspire people like me who get inundated with confusing information about success and failures.

Reference

McCullough, M. E. (1995). Prayer and health: Conceptual issues, research review, and research agenda. *Journal of Psychology and Theology*, *23*(1), 15-29.

10. John Wells: Was it a miracle or Coincidence?

Tuesday 8th May 2012 at 2.30am was the exact time the telephone started to ring.

Just an hour ago, after a week of long hard work, I had been exhausted and yet I had a sense of achievement due to my successful completion of a research project which had to be submitted on the following day. I hit the sack. I have a tendency to put my nose to the grindstone when it comes to accomplishing a project and consequently sleep like a log afterwards. That night was not an exception.

The brittle, yet modulated voice from the other end started to leave a message on the telephone.

'I am extremely sorry Father that I have to ring you at this time of the night - by the way my name is Tabin, daughter of Alice and John Wells. My Father John is ...'

Halfway through her message, I dashed to the phone and picked it up. I interrupted straightaway, apologising for the delay in answering the call. Tabin sounded comforted by my apology and told me of her father's imminent death, she asked if it would be possible for me to join them and pray for her Dad at my earliest convenience.

I assured her of my presence and prayers and asked where their temporary accommodation was. She told me that they were in a Care Home called 'Blackdown' in Mary Tavy near Tavistock.

After my conversation with Tabin, I hurriedly looked for my shoes, socks and clerical attire. As I was putting them on, I started to browse my iPad to find the driving directions to Blackdown Care Home.

It looked straight forward, so I made a note of just the postcode to use on my Satnav in the car.

A generous member of the Parish has previously given me a TOM TOM and, due to its accurate track record, I confidently fed in the postcode for Blackdown Care Home. It estimated that it would only take 19 minutes. I was in the car driving within six minutes of my conversation with Tabin.

Encouraged by the prediction of a short journey, I was confident that

I would reach John in time to offer him the last sacrament before his final repose.

As usual, the Satnav was determining every road and turn. I loved to slavishly follow the instructions because it had never let me down in the past. In addition, I must confess I had not activated the parts of my brain required for map reading skills, as I falsely imagined they required more sophisticated skills and training than I possessed!

Moreover, in the past I have compared the methods of driving in India to those in Britain, and have used my research skills to learn and unlearn both the good and the bad driving habits. There are many good things about driving in India, but the one I found most helpful is that, unlike British destinations, most of the major towns and villages have just one road and therefore getting lost is less likely. On the other hand, one needs to get used to vehicles being driven in the opposite directions and wrong lanes every so often.

'You have reached your destination' my TOMTOM said. I was so happy to get out of my car but my happiness was short lived. To my horror, I could not see any signs of the Blackdown Care Home, 'Instead I saw a cattle-shed with no lights in the middle of no-where. I drove around, desperately looking for some signs of a human dwelling in the area, let alone the care home. My TOMTOM kept repeating, 'turn around where possible,' redirecting me back to the cattle-shed. I did go back a couple of times but made a decision to drive around bit further from that place. The further I drove away the louder was the voice of the redirection. The silvery and singsong voice of the lady in my TOMTOM suddenly started to sound tremulous and toneless. After an hour of driving around, I began to realise that my beloved TOMTOM this time had indeed let me down. It kept insisting every so often to 'turn around where possible,' directing me back to the same cattle-shed.

I began to panic with the horrible thought of missing the opportunity to administer the last sacrament to John as requested by Tabin and the family.

I pulled the car up by the kerb a few miles away from the cattle shed and began impatiently searching for the map which I vaguely remember having thrown into the boot of my car a few years ago.

I took little interest in map reading in those days as I found it unnecessary: a waste of time and effort. This was because I had the luxury of having been told all the required information for travel by my TOMTOM: the current location, nearby fuel stations, where to start when to stop etc.,

Suddenly I spotted a yellow book of maps in the lower right-hand corner of the boot and I felt immensely relieved by the discovery even before opening it.

I was also increasingly aware of the time drain. Opening the map book, to my dismay I found it was 'UK Road Maps and Atlases' which meant it was no good for my purpose at that moment in the middle of Tavistock.

Looking at the digital clock in my car I realised it was already 3.45 am. Yet not letting my hope fade away, I wanted to give it another try, by leaving my car near the cattle shed and taking a walk in the area to have a careful look around.

As I accelerated towards the cattle shed, holding the steering gently as usual, I heard a rather unpleasant squawky noise that I had never heard before. Since I was in the middle of the road, I could not stop to look into it and so I continued to drive on. I heard the same noise again, but my anxious look spotted the exasperating red flash just beneath the steering wheel indicating I was low on fuel. I knew I was getting into serious trouble.

In panic I searched around the pockets of my trousers and coat to find out whether I had brought along my wallet with money. To my horror, I discovered I hadn't. It was just adding fuel to the flames of anxiety.

Feeling dismayed, I felt prompted to give up my efforts to reach John in order to administer the Last Sacrament. I decided to drive back to the presbytery. Looking rapidly in both directions for any signs of a care home, I drove very slowly. As I was the only driver on the road I felt relieved to have been driving at that time of the night.

Approximately three miles away from the cattle shed, in Mary Tavy I spotted the board on my left that read, 'Black Down'. I shouted instantly, 'Thank God almighty!' Leaving the car by the side of the road, I rushed into the care home with the firm hope of seeing John alive.

The carers at reception were anxiously waiting for my arrival and as soon as I rushed in, they escorted me to the room where three of the family members were sitting around John. He was lying very still but alive.

Even before I could start my conversation, Tabin rushed in, apologising profusely for the late- night request to administer the sacrament to her Dad. I intervened and made it clear that I was glad to have been called and reiterated to the family that every Catholic priest would do the same if approached in such a desperate need.

While talking to them, I started to put on my stole and opened the oils stock. As I began the prayers surrounded by the family, the carers too joined in and half-way through, I noticed John making some movements. When I touched him during that short and moving service, I could feel his reaction as an acceptance of the sacrament.

As I came to the end of the service I could see on the faces of the family overwhelming joy, coupled with appreciation and gratitude.

Afterwards, I tried to engage the family with some good thoughts of God's mercy and generosity which I thought would strengthen their efforts to withstand their grief. The family however, especially Tabin, kept repeating how much they were appreciative of my visit. In all humility, although I accepted their recognition of my tortuous expedition, I also kept repeating how marvellous was the helping grace of God that led me to be present with them in their hour of desperation.

After about an hour, around 4.30 am, I left them whilst John was lying still in the bed.

Whilst driving back various thoughts were crossing my mind. Having been awake almost the entire night the emotions of despair, distress, anxiety and stress should have taken their toll on me but surprisingly I did not feel tired or worn out. I felt entirely the opposite: I felt refreshed and rejuvenated. I was happy and content to have carried out my priestly ministry just when it was needed the most. I felt it was such a privilege and gift as a father-priest to offer God's blessings to his children/parishioners at just the right time.

While driving home, the squawky noise I had heard previously sounded again. I noticed it was the default warning about the low fuel level. However, it did not sound as unpleasant as before. My worry was not as intense as before either. As I continued, I was mentally prepared to pull aside and wait for the AA to rescue me in the case of having a completely empty fuel tank. Thankfully no disaster happened until I reached the Presbytery around 5 am.

I thought I must go to bed for at least couple of hours as I knew I had a long day ahead, starting with Mass at 10.00 am and followed by a seminar at 1.00 pm at Exeter University. Trying to sleep was too hard though as my psychological and critical mind was active, fighting to find, if not answers, at least reasonable explanations to all that had happened. My cradle Catholic faith strongly told me that, without a doubt, everything that happened during that night was truly a miracle... but my psychological critical mind argued to seek the difference between miracles and coincidence. And so, I got up from my bed and tried to browse through thousands of books on the topic via the university online library.

Soon though, exhausted by skimming through those texts on my computer, I gave up because nothing I read quenched my thirst for a deeper understanding or a convincing explanation of all that happened during that night. I decided to go down to the church and simply sat asking the Lord for enlightenment. Unfortunately, nothing happened even after a few hours of my stay in the church. After the Mass at 10 am, I narrated the whole episode to all those who came for the Mass.

In sharing the information, I was particularly interested to know how people would define my experience; either as miracle or as coincidence. Almost every person thanked me for what I had done that night, but one person's reply put my mind at rest.

She said, 'For a believer it was a miracle and for a non-believer it was a coincidence. Miracles bring joyful blessings all around but a coincidence does not'.

I thought she spoke God's voice. I felt really certain that all that had happened that night brought joyful blessings to me, as well as to the family in their grief and sadness.

Other titles by the Author

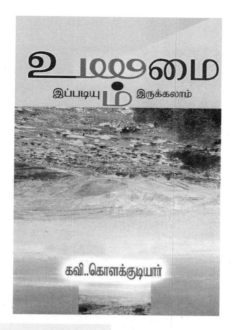

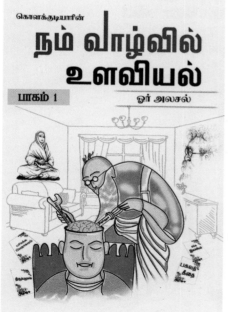

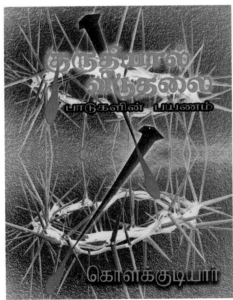

9 781782 229537